The Positive Classroom Field Guide (K-5)

2nd Edition

Muriel K. Rand

Illustrations by Catherine L. Rand

To obtain a FREE pdf copy of this book, please email a copy of your receipt to info@thepositiveclassroom.org

Copyright ©2016 Princeton Square Press. All rights reserved.
Illustrations Copyright ©2012-16 Catherine L. Rand

Published by Princeton Square Press
301 N. Harrison St. No. 312
Princeton, NJ 08536

No part of this publication may be reproduced, stored in a retrieval system, or transmitted in any form or by any means, electronic, mechanical, photocopying, recording, scanning, or otherwise, except as permitted under Section 107 or 108 of the 1976 United States Copyright Act, without either the prior written permission of the publisher, except by a reviewer who may quote brief passages in a review.

ISBN: 978-0-9882766-9-7

Table of Contents

Introduction: The Positive Classroom Method..................3

Part 1: Teaching Classroom Procedures..................5
- How to Teach Procedures..................6
- Effective Transitions..................10
- Procedures Master List..................12
- Teaching Procedures Calendar..................13
- What to Do When Children Don't Follow the Procedures..................21
- Daily Routine and Transitions Templates..................23
- Procedures for Learning Templates..................51

Part 2: Building Classroom Community..................63
- Building Relationships..................64
- Developing Rules..................66
- Morning Meet and Greet..................69
- Monthly Community Building Activities..................77

Part 3: Developing School Success Skills..................113
- Overview..................114
- School Success Skills Curriculum..................115
- Classroom Management Master Calendar..................178

Part 4: Techniques for Engaging Learners..................181
- Engaging Learners..................182
- Planning Learning Centers..................183
- Making Seatwork Successful..................187
- Alternatives to Hand-Raising..................193
- Asking Engaging Questions..................199
- Being Prepared..................201

Part 5: Guiding Behavior..................203
- Guiding Children's Behavior..................204

- Responding to Student Behavior..205
- Positive Teacher Language 206
- Intervening in the Acting Out Cycle...208
- Using a Quiet Corner...210
- Calm Down Kit..211
- Setting and Enforcing Limits..213
- Reducing Attention-Seeking Behavior...215

Summary..218

Introduction
The Positive Classroom Method

The Positive Classroom Method is a five-step plan for developing an elementary classroom in which things run smoothly, there is a positive sense of community, and the children are engaged and learning.

The five steps work together to create a complete classroom management system that is focused on helping K-5 children develop self-control, responsibility, and the necessary social and emotional skills to be successful in school. The 5 steps are:

1. Teaching Classroom Procedures
2. Building Classroom Community
3. Developing School Success Skills
4. Engaging Learners
5. Guiding Behavior

The Positive Classroom Field Guide is a companion to *The Positive Classroom* textbooks. It provides hands-on lessons, activities, posters, teaching cards, and other resources to help you develop classroom management strategies for the first five steps listed above. These resources will save hundreds of hours of work while helping you establish a positive classroom.

In order to be successful in classroom management in elementary school, it is important to use all five of the steps concurrently and focus the first six weeks of school on preventing misbehavior. We wish you all the best throughout the year and we believe The Positive Classroom Method will help you find more joy in teaching!

For more classroom ideas, and to access *The Positive Classroom Method Online Training Course (K-5),* visit:

http://thepositiveclassroom.org/

Part I: Teaching Classroom Procedures

How to Teach Procedures

The first step in teaching procedures is to think through the parts of the day and decide what procedures you want to establish. You can use the list and descriptions of procedures in this manual to get started. Read through the descriptions and adapt them to fit your classroom. Look over the calendar to plan when to teach each procedure.

Next, teach the children each procedure until they know it well enough to do it automatically. Don't think that teaching the procedures once is ever enough. You will need to teach and re-teach them many times, as well as give supportive reminders while children practice them. See the calendar included in this manual for recommendations.

The best way to teach routines is to have the children actually practice them as a lesson. The Responsive Classroom has a wonderful strategy for teaching procedures called Interactive Modeling. There are four steps:

Modeling Procedures

1. You explain why the procedure is important
2. Students observe the model
3. Students describe what's happening
4. Students practice and get immediate feedback

If children are not following the routines, re-teach them and provide more practice. Teachers with the smoothest running classrooms spend the first six weeks of the school year focusing primarily on teaching procedures and developing routines. This time is more than made up for with the increase in efficiency throughout the year.

Interactive Modeling Worksheet

Procedure to be taught: _____

Step 1. Explain why this procedure important

Step 2: Model the procedure

Step 3: Ask what the children noticed about what you modeled

Step 4: Have children practice the procedure and give positive feedback

Step 5: Repeat modeling and noticing if necessary

From Wilson, M.B. (2012). *Interactive modeling: A powerful tool for teaching children.* Turners Falls, MA: Center for Responsive Schools, Inc.

Behavior Anchor Charts

Young children do not understand generalization such as "line up" or "get ready" so your directions need to be put into specific behavioral terms. For example, what exactly do children need to do to "line up"? One way to do this is with the use of a graphic organizer called an Anchor Chart. For example, our chart might look like this:

Lining Up	
Looks Like:	Sounds Like:
• Standing Up • Hands by your side • Stand right behind person in front • Space between people • Face forward	• Quiet • Voice Level 0

You can use Anchor Charts such as this to help the children know exactly what they are expected to do. You can add pictures for younger children or have the children draw the pictures themselves. You can use Anchor Charts as a review of procedures you've already taught by asking the children to come up with the behaviors and fill out the chart.

Behavior

Looks Like	Sounds Like

Effective Transitions

All transitions go more smoothly if children know what to expect. Use interactive modeling to teach each transition. Practice these until the children know what they should be doing and can do it quickly and easily. Here are some tips for making transitions smoother:

Give warnings

This may seem obvious, but sometimes you lose track of the time and try to quickly get children to change what they are doing. Resist this! Stay organized and give the children at least one warning that a transition is coming up—more might be needed for children who have trouble with transitions. You can also use timers to let children know how much time is left before a transition. This can be a personal kitchen timer for an individual child, or a timer posted on your SmartBoard or computer screen which counts down for the whole class.

Use music cues

Music is a powerful way of helping children to know the schedule and the behaviors that are expected at different times. Plan welcome songs to begin the day, clean up songs, soft music before nap quiet activities, and a good-bye song at dismissal.

Actively supervise

During transitions, scan all areas of the room, moving to potential problem areas, making your presence known, and interacting with the children. If you are busy during transitions getting your materials ready for the next activity, talking to other adults in the room, or taking care of administrative work, the children will likely misbehave. Much research over many years has shown that effective teachers have the room and the work ready before school begins.

Allow time for transitions

Young children need plenty of time to figure out where they need to go or what they need to do next. Often teachers plan schedules that reflect the time they need for each activity but not the time between activities. It can take longer than expected to get children to put their things away, get ready to leave the classroom and then walk down the hall. When children are rushed, everyone's anxiety level goes up (including the teacher's) and children are less cooperative.

Move children gradually

Try to stagger the children's movement to the next activity. For example, if you are moving children from group time on the rug to working at their desks, gradually send small groups of children over to begin work. Make sure that young children do not have time during transitions in which they have nothing to do.

Use imagination

Try gaining children's cooperation and interest during transitions by using imagination and dramatic play. Children are quieter when walking down the hall pretending to be little mice. They will enjoy cleaning up when they pretend to be a big dump truck or a large crane that picks up materials. Children will cooperate better when you wave a magic wand that creates quiet voices or makes everyone tip-toe. Creating a joyful attitude during transitions reduces the tension and helps children feel comfortable.

Keep learning

Engage the children in learning activities to keep them focused during transitions. These activities could be counting by 5 or 10, reciting vocabulary words, practicing phonics rules, singing songs, chanting poems or rhymes, and so on. By giving the children something to focus on, they are less likely to wander or be off task during transitions.

Adapt transitions for special needs

Some children with disabilities will need more transitioning time or different procedures than the rest of the class. Children who are highly sensitive to noise and activity may be overwhelmed by the stimuli during transitions. You might want to help the child transition before or after the other children, or to allow the child to wait in a quiet location until the next activity begins. Try visual cues such as reminder cards, photos, and posters and use positive feedback.

Procedures Master List

Daily Routines & Transitions

- Quiet Signal
- Arrival Procedures
- Bathroom Routine (#1, #2, #3)
- Lining Up
- Walking in the Hall
- Sitting at Group Time
- Moving from Desks to Carpet
- Moving from Carpet to Desks
- Voice Levels
- Snack Routine
- Fire Drill//Safety Drills
- Getting a drink
- Sharpening Pencils
- Classroom Jobs
- Dismissal Procedure
- Going to the Nurse

Procedures for Learning

- Sitting in Learner's Position
- Putting Things Away in Your Desk
- Taking a Break During Seatwork
- Using Personal Whiteboards
- Turn and Talk
- Choral Response
- Reader's Workshop
- Read to Self
- Partner Reading
- Listening Center Reading
- Writer's Workshop
- Math Centers
- What to Do When You're Done Early

Teaching Procedures Calendar
Week 1: Basic Procedures

Day 1:

Morning	*Quiet Signal* *Arrival Procedures* *Bathroom Routine*
Mid-Day	Quiet Signal *Lining Up* *Walking in Hallway*
Afternoon	Quiet Signal *Dismissal Procedure*
Make teaching procedures and getting to know the children your primary goal the first week. Do not put out all your materials. Only have available what is needed and cover up any materials you have not introduced yet.	

*New Procedures are in Italics

Day 2:

Morning	Quiet Signal Arrival Procedures Bathroom Routine *Snack Routine (if applicable)*
Mid-Day	Review Quiet Signal Lining Up/ Walking in Hallway
Afternoon	Review Quiet Signal Dismissal Procedure

Day 3:

Morning	Arrival Procedures Snack Routine (if applicable) *Putting Things Away in Your Desk*
Mid-Day	Quiet Signal *Getting a Drink* Lining Up/ Walking in Hallway
Afternoon	Dismissal Procedure
Review Quiet Signal and Bathroom Routine if needed. If the children are following these well, give lots of positive feedback.	

Day 4:

Morning	Quiet Signal Arrival Procedures
Mid-Day	Lining Up/Walking in Hallway
Afternoon	*Sitting at Group Time* Dismissal Procedure
Observe how well the children are following the Quiet Signal, Lining Up/Walking in Hallway, and Bathroom Routine. Reteach if needed. If the children are following these well, give lots of positive feedback. Be sure all children are following procedures correctly.	

Day 5:

Morning	Arrival Procedures *Sitting in Learner's Position* Putting Things Away in Your Desk
Mid-Day	Sitting at Group Time
Afternoon	*Fire Drill Procedure* Dismissal Procedure
Review Quiet Signal, Lining Up/Walking in Hallway, and Bathroom Routine if needed. If the children are following these well, give lots of positive feedback.	

Week 2: Reinforcing Basic Procedures

The first day, review these procedures from the previous week:

- Quiet Signal
- Arrival Procedure
- Bathroom Routine
- Lining Up/Walking in Hallway
- Sitting at Whole Group
- Dismissal Procedure
- Getting a Drink

Be sure these are done correctly. If not, re-teach and have the children practice. Give plenty of positive feedback to those who are behaving correctly.

Introduce the following procedures this week:

- *Voice Levels*
- *Moving from Carpet to Desks*
- *Moving from Desks to Carpet*
- *Going to the Nurse*
- *Sharpening Pencils*
- *Classroom Jobs*

Spend the rest of the week on review of all the procedures taught so far. Spend as much time as needed. DO NOT worry about introducing new curriculum. Review simple lessons and focus 90% of your time and attention on teaching procedures.

Week 3: Learning Procedures

Review any procedures that are not yet smooth. Practice each one of them this week until all children are doing them easily. Keep this fun and light – do not get demanding or children may resist. Use plenty of praise for those who are doing well.

Teach the following new procedures:

- *Using Personal White Boards*
- *Turn and Talk*
- *Choral Response*
- *What to Do When You're Done Early*

Introduce any new materials you haven't used yet. Include math center manipulatives, art materials, or computer software that you will use in your classroom. Teach children how to take out and put away the materials and use them properly. Develop these procedures yourself, since they will vary with what materials you have in your classroom.

Also teach the procedures for *Lock Down/Safety Drills* according to your school's policies.

Week 4: Working Independently

Review the basic Day One Procedures using Interactive Modeling one more time:

- Quiet Signal
- Arrival Procedures
- Bathroom Routine
- Lining Up/Walking in Hallway
- Sitting at Whole Group
- Dismissal Procedure

If you have one or two children who are struggling with certain procedures, work with these children one-on-one. See the next section for what to do if children are not following the routines.

Teach the following new procedures:
- *Reader's Workshop*
- *Read to Self*
- *Partner Reading*
- *Listening Center Reading*
- *Writer's Workshop*
- *Math Centers*
- *Taking a Break During Seatwork*

Week 5: Using Learning Centers

Learning centers are an important instructional strategy to help you individualize instruction. In order to be successful, learning center procedures must be taught systematically before children are able to work independently. This is critical so that you can spend the time when children are at centers conducting small group reading and math lessons and one-on-one consultations with children.

Using the instructions below, plan your learning centers and this week teach the procedures needed. See Step 4: Engaging Learners for more Learning Center templates and signs.

Plan Learning Center Activities

The better prepared you are before center time starts, the smoother things will go. Here's a list of the questions you might consider in your planning to help you figure out what behaviors children need to learn and what you need to have ready before class begins.

Where does each child go?

Think about how children will know where they will go when center time begins. If you are using free choice, you will still want to have a planning time. This can be done in a small group and plans can be written or oral. If you are using assigned centers, create a chart that shows what center they begin with.

What do children do when they get there?

Be clear what activities children will do in each center and how they will use the materials or record what they have done. Next, teach the children the procedures for each and every center. Mini-lessons during group time are one way to show children what is available to them and how to use the materials.

Where do they put their work when they are done?

Children's work can be collected in labeled shelves or bins for each child, a specific folder to put work in, a "center-time journal," or binder.

What do they do if they finish early?

If you are rotating through centers, children will need to have activities available that they can work on if they finish before it's time to move to the next center, or before center time is over. This might be activities that they can get from a specific place, or other follow-up activities that children particularly enjoy.

What do children do if they need help?

Be sure children know what to do if they need help before starting learning centers. Here are some popular strategies:

- **Ask three then me.** Children are taught to ask three other people—peers or adults—for assistance before going to the teacher. You can also designate 1 or 2 people whose job for the week is to help other children with questions. They can wear a badge that says, "ASK ME."

- **Stop sign.** Have a visual signal that shows STOP or DO NOT DISTURB that you can post when you are working with a small group. When children interrupt, point to the sign and gently redirect them to someone else who can help them, or to try on their own. Make it clear that you will not interact with other children while you are working in a "teacher group."

- **Alternative work.** If a child can't figure out how to do a particular question or activity, have an alternative problem, activity, or worksheet that is available. You can also teach children to go to the next problem or step in the activity if they get stuck.

- **Emergencies.** Teach children they can only interrupt you for an emergency and teach them what an "emergency" is. For very young children, role play can help them understand this concept; for example, if someone is hurt or sick, fire, smoke, etc.

- **Out of bounds.** Designate a specific area that is the teacher group area. Mark off the area with tape on the floor and teach the children that it is out of bounds during center time.

How do they know when and where to go to the next activity?

If you have free choice centers, children will be able to move from one activity to the next. However, you might still want them to take a moment to clean up what they were working with, check their center time plans, and possibly record what they have done with a drawing or writing. If you are rotating centers, you will want to give children a warning before it is time to switch centers so that children can emotionally prepare themselves as well as finish up what they've been doing. Then you will need a clear signal for when it is time to change.

Practice these changes between centers so that children can do them quickly and smoothly. Also make sure children know exactly where they go when they rotate centers. This will increase the children's time on task and keep management problems to a minimum.

Week 6: Review All Procedures

Review all basic procedures from Week 1 to ensure they have been turned into automatic routines. Give positive feedback.

Begin using Learning Centers now that you've taught all the procedures. Review any other procedures that are not yet smooth. Break them down into smaller steps if needed and go through modeling and the practice cycle.

Work one-on-one with any children who still need more support. Always assume they CAN'T do the procedure yet, rather than they WON'T do the procedure. This will allow you to stay positive and focus on teaching. Do not punish!

Things should be running smoothly now! Throughout the rest of the year, and especially after holiday breaks, reteach your procedures as needed.

What to Do When Children Don't Follow Procedures

Perhaps you've taught the procedures but some of the children are ignoring your instructions. The first thing to do is to determine how many children are not following the procedures. If it is many children, use STEP 1 below. If it is only 1-3 children, use STEP 2.

STEP 1: Many Children Don't Follow Procedures

The first thing to do is to reteach the procedure. Don't scold them or preach to them. Just reteach the procedure. It's like learning a math skill. If many of the children don't get it, there's no point in scolding them or punishing them. You just need to reteach.

For example, if the children aren't quiet in the hallway, stop them and ask them quietly to return to the classroom. Then say, "I noticed that some of you are having trouble with walking quietly in the hallway so let's go over that again. Who can show us how to walk in the hall? If you can, pick a child who was misbehaving to model this. "What did you all notice?" Have a couple of children describe what they saw. Now let's practice this again. Take them into the hallway and practice. Halfway down the hall, stop them and praise the children who did it well. For now, ignore those who still misbehaved. This will show the children that you are serious about your procedure and will back it up. It will also help those children who really didn't fully learn the procedure the first time.

STEP 2: One or Two Children Don't Follow Procedures

If there are only one or two children who don't follow the procedure, you'll want to work with them individually. During seatwork, center time, snack or other free time, pull them aside. Say, "Michael, I've noticed you're having trouble walking correctly in the hallway and I want to help you." Let's spend some time practicing. Can you show me the right way to walk in the hall?" It's critical that you keep your voice neutral or positive - even if you're incredibly frustrated. If you show you are angry, the children might dig in their heels and fight against you. The trick is to stay POSITIVE and show the child you REALLY want to help. Have the child walk in the hall and give lots of positive feedback.

Here's an important trick: The next time the whole class walks in the hallway, be sure to focus your POSITIVE attention on this child. "Wow, Michael, you did a great job today of staying quiet and walking along the wall." Too often children get lots of attention when they don't follow the procedures. We get frustrated with these kids and blow up: "Michael, how many times do I have to tell you to stay in line and be quiet? What's the matter with you?" Instead, if you want to change their behavior quickly, just give them lots of sincere praise when they do the procedure appropriately. This takes a lot of our own self-control and professionalism!

Daily Routines and Transitions Templates

Quiet Signal

1. Stop

2. Look at the teacher

3. Put down anything in your hands

4. Keep voice silent (level 0)

5. Keep eyes on teacher

Tips: Use a short, clear auditory signal to quiet the children. A bell or chime works much better than clapping or hand signals. You want a sound that cuts through any chatter and is clear and precise.

Arrival Procedures

1. Come into the classroom and walk over to the coat hooks.

2. Look around and make sure there is space between you and the other children.

3. Take off your coat and hang it on the hook.

4. Bring book bag to desk. Take out any papers for the teacher and put them on the corner of your desk.

5. Sit down and look at the board for "Do Now" work.

6. Begin working.

Tips: Adapt this as necessary depending on the layout of your room, your storage facilities for children's things, and what kinds of items the children have to put away.

Bathroom Routine #1

1. Check the sign to see if you may use the bathroom without asking.

2. Check to make sure the bathroom chart is empty.

3. Get up quietly. Put your name tag on the clip for Girls Bathroom or Boys Bathroom.

4. Leave the room quietly.

5. When you return, remove your name tag from the chart.

6. Sit down quickly and quietly.

7. If the bathroom chart is full and you have an emergency, raise your hand.

Tips: Create a chart with two sections for Boys and Girls. Add a stick-on clip to each side. Create name tags for children that they keep in their desk.

Boys' Bathroom

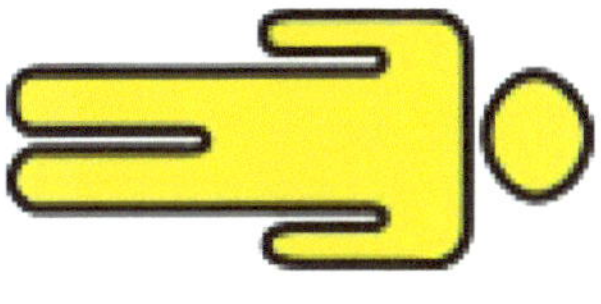

Girls' Bathroom

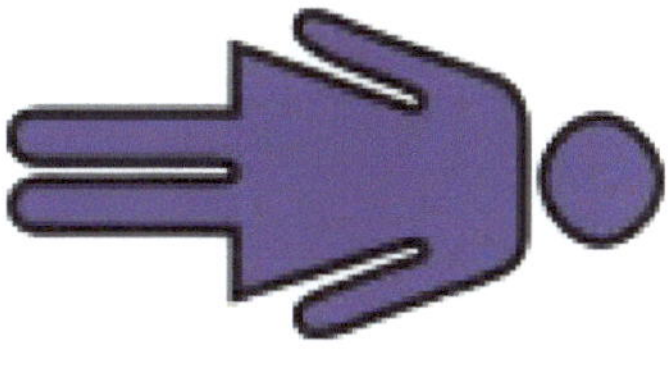

Bathroom Routine #2

1. Check the sign to see if you may use the bathroom without asking.

2. Get up quietly and walk to the sign-out journal. Sign your name and the time.

3. Leave the room quietly.

4. When you return, sign in again.

5. Sit down quickly and quietly.

Tips: Use the signs on the next page. Put up the appropriate sign during your lesson. Create a sign out sheet or journal and find an appropriate place to keep it so the children are not disruptive when they sign out. Younger children can just sign their name without the time.

You may use the bathroom without asking

Please wait to use the Bathroom

Hold up 2 fingers for an emergency

Bathroom Routine #3

1. Check the sign to see if the bathroom is occupied.

2. If the bathroom is empty, get up quietly and walk to bathroom.

3. When you return sit down quickly and quietly.

Tips: Choose which bathroom routine you want to use. #3 is designed for classrooms that have a bathroom in the room. Use the signs below to show "Occupied" or "Available".

Available

Occupied

Lining Up

1. Walk quickly and safely to the line.

2. Face forward.

3. Stand with your hands at your sides.

4. Keep mouth closed. Voice level 0.

5. Move when prompted.

Tips: For younger children, it is very helpful to mark the floor with tape or decals to show them where to stand. You can call children in smaller groups ("everyone at the green table,") or you can establish a permanent order to the line and use that order every time (alphabetical, or assign children numbers).

Walking in the Hallway

1. Line up in order.
2. Stay in Line.
3. Hands to your side.
4. Voice Level 0.
5. Greet friends with wave only, no voice.
6. Hold the door for the person behind you.

Tips: Establish a line order and keep it the same all year. This reduces confusion and fighting about where they are in line.

Sitting at Group Time

1. Sit down right away.

2. Make sure there is space around you.

3. Cross your legs.

4. Track the speaker.

5. Keep hands and body in your own space.

Tips: Make sure there is enough room on the carpet so that children are not touching each other. Use carpet squares or tape to mark off each child's personal space.

Moving from Desks to Carpet

1. Put away books and papers in your desk.

2. Stand up.

3. Move to the left.

4. Push in your chair.

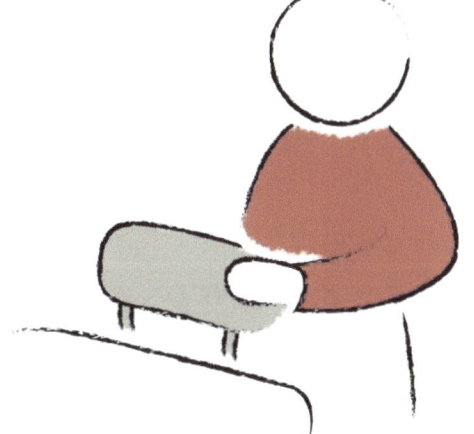

5. Walk down the aisle to the carpet.

6. Find your spot on the carpet.

7. Sit down crossed-legged.

8. Eyes on speaker.

9. Voice silent (level 0) or Participate in Chant.

Tips: Plan the route that each child will take to get to the carpet. Teach each child his or her route. You can use this transition time to chant a song that will teach them spelling patterns, math rules, counting by 5's, etc.

Moving from Carpet to Desks

1. Stand up.

2. Wait to be called.

3. Follow your route to your desk.

4. Sit down.

5. Keep eyes on teacher.

6. Voice level 0 or Participate in Chant.

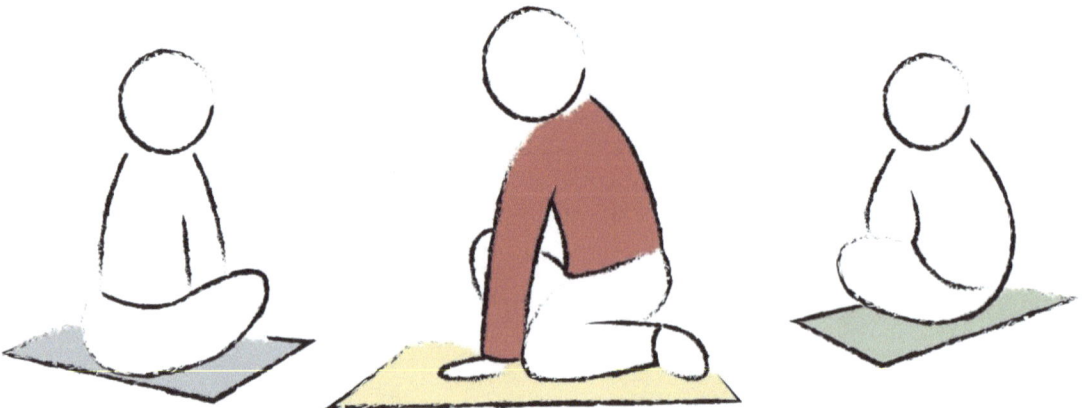

Tips: Plan the route that each child will take to get to the carpet. Teach each child his or her route. You can use this transition time to chant a song that will teach them spelling patterns, math rules, counting by 5's, etc.

Voice Levels

Tips: Use the poster below to teach children the different voice levels.

1. Model what each level sounds like and have the children practice that level. Children need to know what it *feels like* at each voice level.

2. Before starting an activity, use a paperclip or clothespin to mark what level is expected during each lesson.

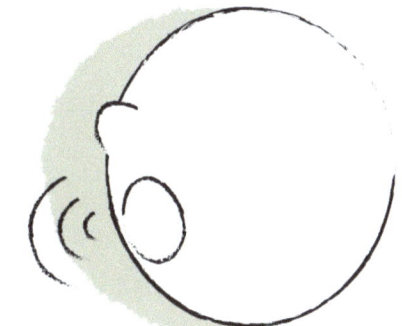

3. As the children are working, point out the children who are using the appropriate voice level.

4. At the end of the activity, ask the children to give a thumbs up or thumbs down in front of their chests to evaluate how well they stayed at the appropriate voice level.

5. Do not nag! If children get too loud, simple ring your chime and remind the whole class of the appropriate voice level. Remember to point out who is doing a good job!

Voice Levels

4	outside
3	speaker voice
2	group talk
1	whisper
0	silent

Snack Routine

1. Get snack from backpack when called.

2. Keep all food to yourself. Do not share (because of allergies).

3. Raise hand if you need help opening items.

4. Voice level 2.

5. Clean up all snack items.

6. Get focused and ready to learn.

Tips: Adapt this routine for your own setting, especially if the school provides snack. It's important to allow chatting during snack so that the children get their social needs met.

Fire Drill Routine

1. When alarm sounds, stand up.

2. Put down all materials and get in line.

3. Walk silently in the hallway and out of the front door.

4. Stop at our safety spot.

5. Wait silently until told to return.

6. Walk silently back to class.

7. Resume your work.

Tips: It is best to teach your lining up procedure and walking in the hallway procedure *before* the fire drill routine. Adapt this procedure for Lock-Down Drills according to your school's procedure. Lock-Down Drills should be taught in a calm manner. Emphasize the importance of always following the teacher's instructions.

Getting a Drink

1. Drinks are allowed once during snack time, and once during seatwork.

2. Quietly walk to the fountain.

3. Take a drink while counting to five.

4. When you get to five, return to class.

5. Get right back to work.

Tips: If allowed by your school, have each child bring a water bottle that they can keep on their desk. Otherwise, designate a few times during the day that the children can get a drink and allow it only during those times. Don't require anyone to ask permission; instead, teach them the procedures and establish trust. If children abuse this process, you can regulate their behavior by giving them one or two "drink tickets" they must hand in to get a drink.

Sharpening Pencils

1. If you need a sharpened pencil, walk over to the pencil box.

2. Put your pencil in the "Please Sharpen" box.

3. Take a pencil from the "Ready to Write" box.

4. Return quietly to your seat.

Tips: Gather two cups or cans that fit pencils. Label one "Please Sharpen." Label the other "Ready to Write." Start off the year with a dozen or so pencils in the sharpened box. Assign one of your classroom jobs to be Pencil Sharpener. At the end of the day, that helper can sharpen all the pencils in the "Please Sharpen" box.

Pencil Container

Ready to Write

Please Sharpen

Classroom Jobs

1. When job time begins, check the chart for your job.

2. Read the task card for your job and follow the directions.

Tips: Create a job chart with spaces to put the children's names. You can rotate them monthly. Some jobs to consider are: Pencil Sharpener, Plant Caretaker, Library Helper, Trash Collector, Whiteboard/Chalkboard Cleaner, AV Specialist, "Ask Me" Helper, Desk Inspector, Messenger, Computer Helper, Supplies Organizer, and Substitutes for anyone who is absent. You can establish 10 minutes at the end of the day for jobs to be completed.

For each job, create a task card that explains the procedure to use for that job. Print and laminate the cards. Give lots of positive feedback for completing jobs appropriately.

Dismissal Routine

1. When called, get your backpack and coat.

2. Gather materials needed for homework. Put them in your backpack.

3. Put on your coat, if needed.

4. Put chair upside down on desk.

5. Stand by your desk and wait to be called to line up.

Tips: Adapt this procedure to your classroom situation.

Procedures for Learning Templates

Sitting in Learner's Position

1. Sit up straight.

2. Feet on the floor.

3. Hands on the desk.

4. Face the speaker.

5. Track the speaker.

Tips: Teach children to "track" the speaker by having them make eye contact with the speaker at all times. This increases their ability to pay attention.

Putting Things Away in Your Desk

1. Look in your desk.

2. If necessary, move things around to make room for the item.

3. Put in the item gently.

4. Make sure that no papers are falling out.

5. Check the photo to see if your desk is neat.

Tips: Create a plan for where each child's books, folders, and writing materials go in their desks. Take a photo of a desk organized properly. Enlarge the photo and post it so the children can use it as a reference. If a few children have trouble staying organized, tape a smaller photo on their desk for them to refer to.

Taking a Break during Seatwork

1. If you are having trouble focusing, take one break.

You can:
- Get a drink
- Stand and stretch
- Close your eyes and think of your happy place
- Go look out the window

2. After one minute, go back to your desk and start working again.

3. Keep working, even if it's hard.

Tips: Decide for yourself what is an appropriate break in your classroom. These are just suggestions. Model for the children how to take a break. Have a clock available so they can keep track of one minute. Some children might need a timer.

Using a Dry Erase Board

1. Take out your board.

2. Take out your marker.

3. Take out your wiping cloth.

4. Write on your board the way the teacher tells you to. Write gently.

5. When done, make sure the marker has a cap on it tightly.

6. Put everything back in your desk.

Tips: If there is not room in the desks for the whiteboards, keep them in one location and have children go in small groups to get a board.

Turn and Talk

1. Sit "Shoulder to Shoulder" with your partner.

2. Look at your partner.

3. One friend talks; one friend listens.

4. Switch. ⇆

Tips: The turn and talk procedure must be taught and practiced before you try this strategy. Be sure the children know ahead of time who their partner is. Keep the time they talk very short so they don't get off track. See Part 4 of the No-Fail Guide to Classroom Management for more ideas about Turn and Talk.

Choral Response

1. The teacher asks a question.

2. Think of your answer.

3. Wait for the signal. Do not raise your hand.

4. Everyone responds on the signal.

Tips: Practice this a few times before using it. Be sure you have a hand signal, like an orchestra conductor, so they know when to respond.

Reader's Workshop: Read to Self

1. When called, get your books.

2. Find a smart place to read away from other children.

3. Stay in your spot the whole time.

4. Get started right away.

5. Read to yourself the whole time.

6. Voice Level 0.

7. Put books away when done.

Tips: Younger children may need to whisper read to help fluency and accuracy. Spend time teaching them how to choose a smart spot for reading. Teach them how to choose a book that is just right for their level.

Reader's Workshop: Partner Reading

1. When called, get your book bag from the shelf.

2. Meet your partner and choose a smart spot to read. Stay in this spot the whole time.

3. Sit close together.

4. Choose who will read first and begin right away.

5. After reading, the listener asks the reader to retell the story and listens carefully. Switch roles.

6. Read and retell for the whole time.

7. Put books away when done.

Tip: Model this procedure for the children many times and have them practice how to sit, how to take turns, and how to retell the story to their partner.

Reader's Workshop: Listening Center Reading

1. When called, move to the listening center.

2. Choose an appropriate book.

3. Put on headphones and begin listening right away.

4. Follow along with the words and pictures.

5. Listen to reading the whole time.

6. Start a new story if there is time.

7. Put materials away.

Tips: Have all books, CDs, iPod, or computer program set up before you start reader's workshop. You can assign this to students as their weekly job.

Writer's Workshop

1. Get out your writing folder.

2. Take out the writing piece you are working on. Read it.

3. Begin writing. Work on the skill you have been assigned.

4. Keep going, even when it is hard. Write the whole time.

5. Voice level 0.

6. Put away your folder when you are done.

Tips: Be sure each child has personal goals to work on for their writing. Establish these goals as you conference with each child.

Math Stations

1. Check the Math Station Chart to see where you will go.
2. When you are called, move quickly to your station.
3. Read the directions.
4. Begin working right away.
5. Stay at your station the whole time.
6. Put all materials away.
7. Move to the next station.

Tips: Have enough math stations so that there are only 3-4 children at each station. Create a chart with pictures of each station. Rotate children's names weekly for each station.

Part 2: Building Classroom Community

Building Relationships

Do you want to create an amazing classroom in which the children are well-behaved and learning – and you are enjoying teaching? Building relationships is the key to achieving this.

If we want children to follow our rules and behave in class, it is critical that they feel like they belong and are cared about. Over the years, I've watched many children misbehave in incredibly creative ways. One boy picked up an armful of the teacher's things off her desk and threw them out the window. One girl crawled under her desk whenever seatwork started. Some children poke, pester, and annoy the other children. Some call out all day long. Some wander around the room, and some get belligerent and shout back when asked to work.

And you know what all these behaviors have in common? These children got the teacher's attention and the children's attention. Many children come to school today starved for attention. Some of our children's needs for love and belongingness are not being met. We need to create a classroom that meets these needs. If you don't want to be frustrated and exhausted at the end of the day, you need to build classroom community. It's THAT important!

Two Kinds of Relationships

There are two kinds of relationships that need to be fostered in your classroom. The first is the relationship between you and the kids. Most teachers do this pretty well and many elementary school teachers decided to go into teaching because they love children and want to have a good relationship with them.

The second kind of relationship is helping children develop positive relationships with *each other*. You'll want to offer many activities that help children to get to know one another, and activities that help you all feel like you are part of a "family." The section that follows includes activities that you can use throughout the school year to develop positive relationships in your classroom. By carrying out these activities you will be *preventing* misbehaviors such as teasing, tattling, bullying, and attention-seeking. In addition to building relationships, you'll also create a positive climate.

Build a Positive Relationship with Children

- Greet each child warmly every day.

- Ask children about their life outside of school—what they do at home, etc.

- Get to know something personal about each child that you can talk about.

- Watch children's TV shows and be able to talk to children about the shows.

- Let children talk to you about their feelings without being judgmental.

- Get to know the children's families. Include multicultural books in your library representing the cultures of your children.

- Spend a few minutes as often as you can individually talking to a child.

- If you are angry with a child, wash the slate clean at the end of the day and let him or her know you are starting over again fresh the next day.

- Let children know they are missed when they are absent.

- Put up photos of the children's families.

- Provide positive feedback as often as possible throughout the day, aiming for 5 times more positive comments than negative ones.

Developing Rules

In order to get children to follow the rules in the classroom, they need to feel like they *belong*. The reason why any of us follow rules is because we feel a part of the community that developed the rules. Children who misbehave often feel like outsiders and they don't feel like they are part of the community. Start developing the rules in your classroom during the first week (but not the first day) after you have some of the basic procedures done.

Here are the steps for getting children involved in developing the rules for their classroom:

1. Gather them together and have them turn and talk to a friend about what a good classroom would look like and feel like.

2. Ask children what rules would be needed to create that good classroom. Write down their ideas.

3. Review the children's ideas and eliminate any that are not appropriate.

4. Hel the children group their ideas into categories. Try to make the categories relate to these three ideas:

    a. We are good to others

    b. We are good to ourselves

    c. We are good to our materials

5. Write your 3 rules down, or use the poster on the following page.

6. Have the children sign the rules to show they understand them and promise to follow them.

7. Refer to the rules frequently, teaching the children what they mean.

Morning Meet & Greet

Plan about 15-20 minutes every morning in which your entire class gathers and greets each other. It's best if children can sit in a circle or around the edge of a carpet so they can see each other. Here's an outline for the meeting:

1. Welcome from the teacher (1 minute)
2. Greeting – children greet each other (5-10 minutes)
3. Morning message and classroom news. (5 minutes)
4. Group activity such as song, storytelling, shared writing lesson, etc. (5 minutes)

These greetings are so important because the fulfill children's need for attention and their desire to fit in and be part of a group. They teach very important social skills that some children will not yet have learned. Most importantly, they help the whole class start the day in a positive, caring way.

On the next few pages are a variety of options for conducting morning greetings. Try them out and discover which ones work best in your classroom.

Handshake Greeting

Children sit in circle. The first person (let's call her Jennifer) turns and faces the next child (Sam). The two children make eye contact and shake hands. Jennifer says, "Good Morning, Sam." Then Sam says, "Good morning, Jennifer." Then Sam turns to the next person in the circle and repeats the greeting. The greeting goes completely around the circle. For times when germs are a problem, children can get silly and touch elbows or gently fist bump.

High-Five Greeting

Children sit in circle. The first person (let's call her Jennifer) turns and faces the next child (Sam). The two children make eye contact and Sam holds up his hand. Jennifer gives him a gentle High-Five and says, "Good Morning, Sam." Then Sam says, "Good morning, Jennifer." Then Sam turns to the next person in the circle (Michael). Michael holds up his hand and Sam gives a gentle High-Five and repeats the greeting. The greeting goes completely around the circle. Children must learn to be gentle.

Picture Greeting

Take a picture of each child. Glue or tape the photos onto index cards. Punch holes in the cards and put them on a binder ring. Children sit in a circle. The first person (Jennifer) stands up and takes the ring of cards. She turns to the first card and figures out whose picture it is. She walks over to that child (Sam) and says, "Good Morning, Sam." Then Sam says, "Good morning, Jennifer." Then Jennifer sits down where Sam was and Sam takes the ring of photos and turns to the next picture.

Sam identifies who the next picture is and greets that child. If someone is absent, the child says, "We miss you, _____" and goes to the next picture. This continues until all children are greeted.

Sign Language Greeting

Children sit in circle. The first person (Jennifer) turns and faces the next child (Sam). The two children make eye contact and Jennifer makes the sign for "Hello." Then Sam signs, "Hello." Then Sam turns to the next person in the circle and repeats the greeting. The greeting goes completely around the circle.

Whisper Greeting

Children sit in circle. The first person (Jennifer) turns and faces the next child (Sam). The two children make eye contact and Jennifer whispers "Good Morning" in Sam's ear. Then Sam whispers back "Good Morning" in Jennifer's ear. Then Sam turns to the next person in the circle and repeats the greeting. The greeting goes completely around the circle.

Ball Greeting

Children sit in a circle. The first person takes the ball and rolls it to someone across the circle from her while she says good morning to that child. The receiver then passes it to someone else, saying "good morning." Repeat this until everyone has had a turn.

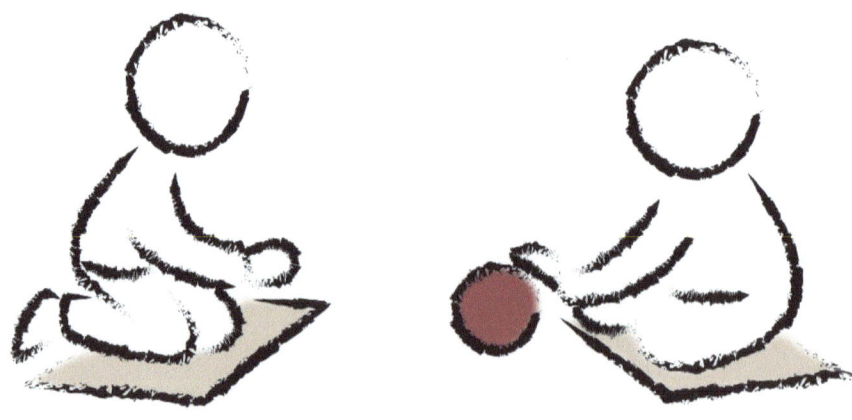

Greetings around the World

Teach the children how to say "good morning" or "hello" in a few different languages. The first person, Jennifer, turns to her neighbor Sam and says the greeting in another language. Sam says the greeting back in the same language. Then he turns to the next person and chooses a different language to greet his neighbor. Repeat this until everyone has had a turn.

- Hola (OH-la) is hello in Spanish.
- Konichiwa (koh-Nee-chee-wah) is hello in Japanese.
- Sabaḥu Al-khair (*sah-bah-heu ahl-kha-ir*) is good morning in Arabic
- Jambo (JAHM-bo) is hello in Swahili.
- Ni hao (nee-Ha-OW) is hello in Chinese.
- Bonjour (bohn-Zhoor) is good morning in French.
- Buon giorno (bwohn-JOR-noh) is good morning in Italian.
- Annyong ha shimnikka (An-YOH HASHim-ni-kah) is hello in Korean.
- Zdravstvuite (ZzDRAST-vet-yah) is hello in Russian.

Snowball Greeting

Gather enough scrap paper for each child to write his or her name on a piece, then crumple it into a "snowball." Separate the children into two lines facing each other and have them toss the snowballs at each other. Then each child picks up a snowball, opens it up, and greets the person whose name is on the paper.

Book Character Greeting

Give the children an index card for them to draw and write the name of a book character. At morning circle, the children holds up their card and use the characters' names for greetings instead of their own names.

Match Greeting

Beforehand, make two sets of index cards that match. For example, one could be numbers and the other set addition sentences (7 on one card, 3+4 on the other card). Pass out the cards to the class. Children find the person that has their match and then they greet each other.

Here are more ideas:
- Upper and lower case alphabet
- Synonyms
- Characters and book titles
- Color swatches and color names
- Pictures of objects and first letter of the word
- Compound words; first and second part on different cards
- Math equation on one card, correct answer on another card

1-Minute Greeting

Children stand up. Set the timer for one minute. Children greet as many other children as they can in one minute. You can use handshake, high-five, or other types of greetings. When the time is up, use your quiet signal to let children know they should sit down in the circle.

Squeeze Greeting

This is a quick greeting when you are short on time. Everyone holds hands in a circle. The first child smiles at his/her neighbor and squeezes his/her hand. Then the child passes the squeeze and smile to the next person until it goes quickly around the circle. Be sure to practice how to give a gentle squeeze so the children develop self-control.

Monthly Community Building Activities

Building Positive Community

The follow section provides a year's worth of community-building activities. These are in addition to Morning Meet & Greet which should be done every day of the year. Carry out one or more of the following activities every week in September. After that, use the rest of these activities at least once a month to keep your community solid. If children start to bicker, pick on each other, tattle or tease, add more community-building activities. The schedule below is just a suggestion. Feel free to pick and choose from these activities.

Activity Calendar

September
- All About Me Posters
- Classmate BINGO
- Focus Student of the Day
- Classmate Survey: Getting to Know You

October
- Classroom Spirit
- Class T-Shirts
- Name Games

November
- Who Am I?
- We are Grateful Class Book
- Comic Strip Fun

December
- What Do We Have in Common?
- Secret Handshake
- Holidays at Home

January
- Our Favorite Things
- How Are We Doing?
- Crazy Collaborative Creatures

February
- Puzzle Piece Valentine's Game
- Musical Hula Hoops
- Back-to-Back Drawing

March
- Reader's Theater
- Inside/Outside Circles
- We're All Superheroes

April
- Partner Obstacle Course
- Pat on the Back
- The Wave

May
- What's the Difference?
- How Does Your Garden Grow?
- Parachute Games

June
- End-of-Year Class Book
- End-of-Year Award Ceremony
- End-of-Year Read-Alouds

September

All about Me Posters

You can substitute this activity for a writing lesson. The children answer the questions about themselves and then hang them up around the room.

See the poster included below.

Classmate BINGO

Use the BINGO game board below. In each square there is a description that might fit the children in your class, such as "Comes to School on the Bus." Give children clipboards with the BINGO sheet. Have them talk to each other and try to find a child's name to match each square. The child should write his or her name in the appropriate square. See sheet below.

Focus Student of the Day

For the first month or so of school, choose one child to be the Focus Student of the Day. Everyone should get a turn and this should not be earned. It's important that even the children who are having behavior problems still get a turn to be accepted and acknowledged. Do not take this away if a child misbehaves. The goal of this activity is for the rest of the class to get to know the Focus Student better and to show that everyone is valued.

Here are some ideas for recognizing the Focus Student:

- Poster about the Star Student
- Lunch with the Teacher
- Line Leader
- Brings in or picks out favorite book for read aloud time
- Brings in show & tell item from home

At Morning Meeting, introduce the Focus Student of the Day. Fill out and create the poster about the student by interviewing him or her during your group meeting. Use the poster below or create your own larger version. At the end of the week you can leave the poster in the room if you have plenty of wall space, or send it home as a souvenir.

B	I	N	G	O
Walks to school	Likes the color blue	Is left handed	Owns a pet	Is wearing sneakers
Likes soccer	Likes to read books	Has brown eyes	Has a younger sibling	Went to the beach this summer
Has a brother	Favorite season is summer	☺ FREE SPACE	Speaks another language besides English	Takes the bus to school
Lives with a grandparent	Has long hair	Likes to sing	Favorite subject in math	Likes to watch TV
Likes to play video games	Has the same birthday month as me	Ate cereal for breakfast	Likes to go to the movies	Just moved to this area

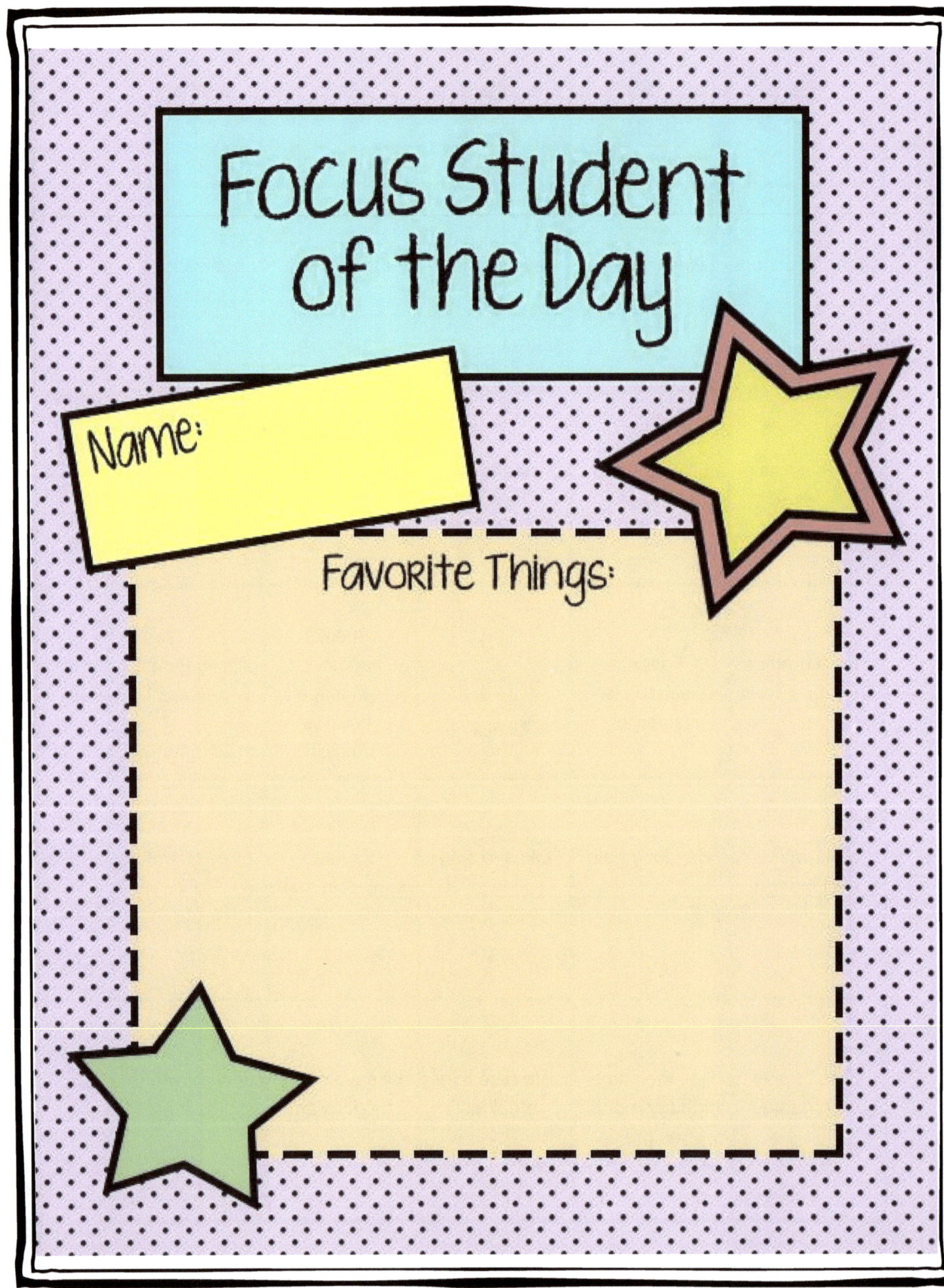

Classmate Survey: Getting to Know You

PreK-1st Grade:

During center time, you can interview one or two children each day. Then read their responses to the whole group during Circle Time. Post the papers on a bulletin board for parents to enjoy.

2nd-5th Grade:

Each student can interview another student and write down his or her responses. Later in the day (or on another day), each student can introduce their partner to the rest of the class by reading their responses.

Getting to Know You

1. What's your name? _____

2. How old are you? _____

3. When is your birthday? _____

4. What's your favorite food?

   _____

5. What do you like to do in school?

   _____

6. What do you like to do at home?

   _____

7. What else would you like people to know about you?

   _____

   _____

   _____

October

Classroom Spirit

Choose a name for your classroom community, a class song, class colors, and a mascot. Use these the way sports teams would during your community celebrations and morning meetings. Combine classroom spirit with your classroom celebrations. Use the sheet below to help children generate ideas and then have them vote for their classroom spirit items.

Class T-Shirts

Ask all the children to bring in a clean white t-shirt. Have all the children write their names on everyone's shirts with a permanent marker. Children can wear their class t-shirts on Friday's throughout October or for other special events.

Name Games

1. Duck, Duck, Goose Name Chase

Play by the standard rules for Duck, Duck, Goose, but instead, the child who is "It" says the name of each child (instead of "Duck") as they go around the circle.

2. Name Dances

Form a circle. Each child chooses a dance movement or action to go with their name. The whole group copies the movements. Repeat until everyone has a chance.

CLASSROOM SPIRIT!

Write your ideas for the following class spirit items:

Class Name:
_____

Class Color:
_____

Class Mascot:
_____

Class Song:
_____

November

Who am I?

Procedure 1: The children will dictate or write something about themselves privately during the day (see form below). Then at group time, you can read each description without telling the name. The children will play a guessing game to figure out who you are describing.

Procedure 2: Children draw pictures that describe themselves (see form below). Next the children tape or pin the pictures on their chests, walk around and give everyone a chance to look at each other's' pictures. Pictures are then shuffled and participants are asked to identify the person to whom the picture belongs.

Who Am I?

We Are Grateful Class Book

1. Review the meaning of the word "grateful."

2. Read a book about being grateful.

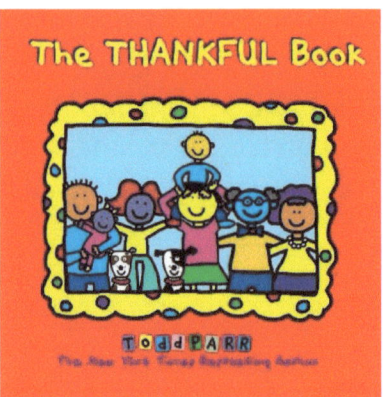

    Preschool: *Be Grateful Little Bear*, by Karen Evelyn-McNeil

                      The Thankful Book by Todd Parr

    Primary: *Grateful Jake* by Emily Madill

                      The Giving Tree by Shel Silverstein

                      Andy and the Lion by James Henry Daugherty

    Elementary: *Thanks a Million* by Nikki Grimes

                      Thanksgiving Day: A Time to Be Thankful by Elaine Landau

3. Have each child complete the following sheet, "I Am Grateful".

4. Publish the completed sheets together into a class book. Read the book to the class.

5. Celebrate being a community and being grateful for each other.

Comic Strip Fun

     Before class, find a few different comic strips appropriate for children and cut each one into boxes. Next pass out the individual boxes to the children and have them find who has the other pieces to their comic strip. When they've found their group members, they should get in order. When everyone is done, have the group read the comic to the rest of the group, or tell a story about the pictures in the comic strip.

December

What Do We Have in Common?

Put the children into groups or 3 or 4. The game begins by having each group figure out how many things they have in common. Younger children can focus on hair color, what they are wearing, or other simple ideas. Older children can focus on what they like, where they live, favorite books, favorite subjects, birthdays, etc.

See the worksheet below to help them record their ideas.

Secret Handshake

Create a secret handshake to use during your morning meet and greet. Children can offer suggestions and you can have the children vote which handshake they want. Encourage the children to keep the handshake secret as their special connection to each other.

Holidays at Home

Invite the children's family members to come to your class to share some items that they use during holiday celebrations. Take photos and create a "Holidays at Home" bulletin board. Children can also make a class book in which they each create a page about a celebration they do at their home. Children who don't celebrate holidays in December can write about what they do with their family in winter.

What Do We Have In Common?

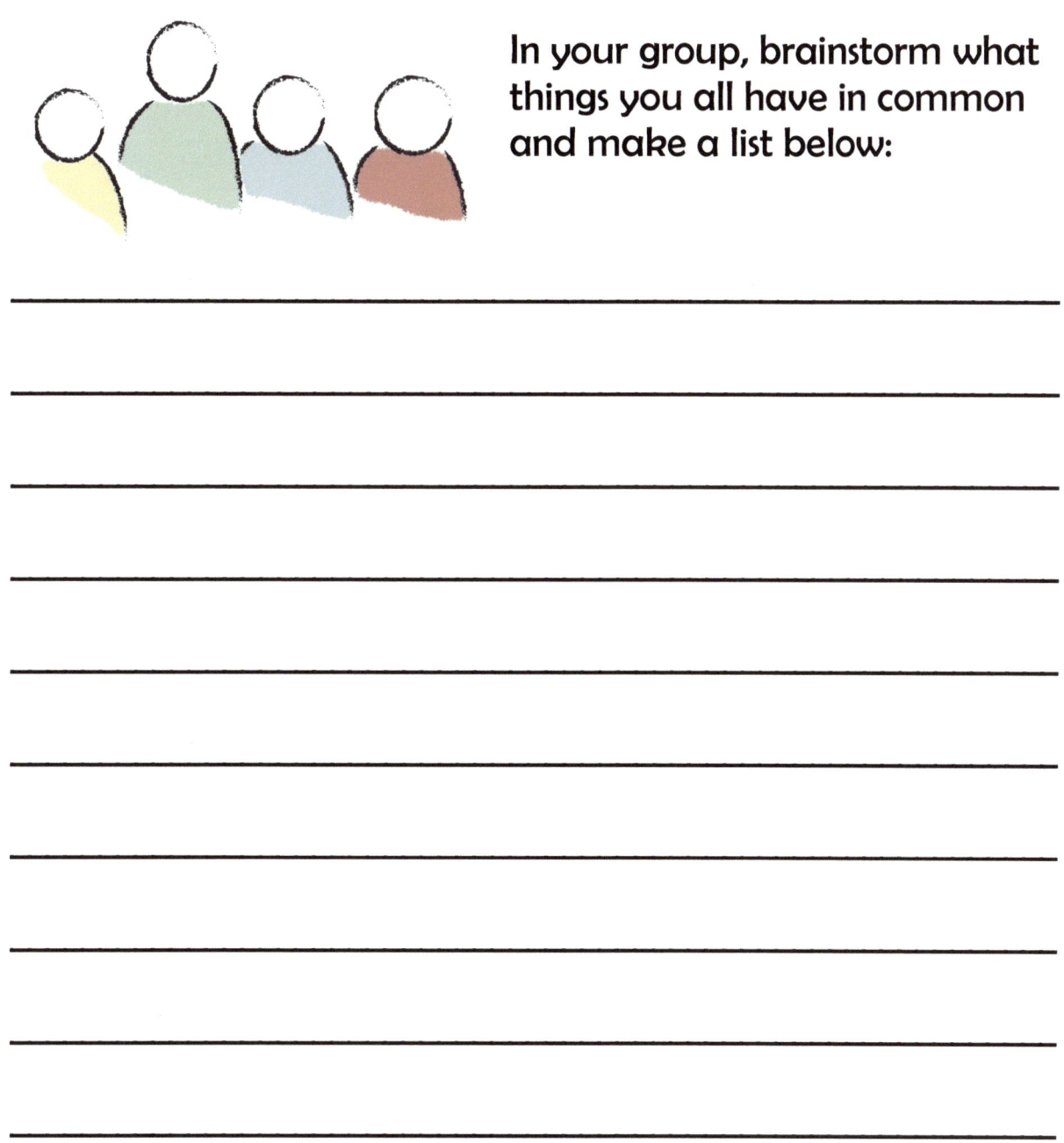

In your group, brainstorm what things you all have in common and make a list below:

_____

_____

_____

_____

_____

_____

_____

_____

What Do We Have In Common?

In your group, figure out how you are alike and draw pictures below:

HOLIDAYS AT HOME

My Family Celebration:

January

Our Favorite Things

Listen to the music: "My Favorite Things" from The Sound of Music. For children who are able to read fluently, you can also print out the lyrics (see below). Have a discussion about the children's favorite things.

Next, as a writing lesson, have the children write about their favorite things. Compile all their essays into a class book. Have one or more of the children add drawings to the cover of the book.

For preschool and kindergarten, you can take dictation and have the children create a picture of their favorite things. For elementary grades, the children can write and illustrate their texts, using narrative, explanatory, or persuasive writing. Be sure to add a page for yourself!

My Favorite Things

Raindrops on roses and whiskers on kittens
Bright copper kettles and warm woollen mittens
Brown paper packages tied up with strings
These are a few of my favorite things

Cream colored ponies and crisp apple strudels
Doorbells and sleigh bells and schnitzel with noodles
Wild geese that fly with the moon on their wings
These are a few of my favorite things

Girls in white dresses with blue satin sashes
Snowflakes that stay on my nose and eyelashes
Silver white winters that melt into springs
These are a few of my favorite things

When the dog bites, when the bee stings
When I'm feeling sad
I simply remember my favorite things
And then I don't feel so bad

Raindrops on roses and whiskers on kittens
Bright copper kettles and warm woolen mittens
Brown paper packages tied up with strings
These are a few of my favorite things

Cream colored ponies and crisp apple strudels
Doorbells and sleigh bells and schnitzel with noodles
Wild geese that fly with the moon on their wings
These are a few of my favorite things

Girls in white dresses with blue satin sashes
Snowflakes that stay on my nose and eyelashes
Silver white winters that melt into springs
These are a few of my favorite things

When the dog bites, when the bee stings
When I'm feeling sad
I simply remember my favorite things
And then I don't feel so bad

My Favorite Things

How Are We Doing?

Discuss the goals you set in the beginning of the year for having a positive classroom and learning together as a community. Review your class rules. Then ask the children to think about how well the class is doing. Give out the following handout and have the children write or draw what the class is doing well and what could be better. When done, share everyone's ideas and list the most common suggestions on chart paper. Refer to the list every once in a while over the next few weeks to check on how things are improving. See handout below.

HOW ARE WE DOING?

☺ **Things our class is doing well:**

☹ **Things we need to improve:**

Crazy Collaborative Creatures

Put the children into groups of three. Give them each a piece of folded paper. See the pattern on the next page. One child draws the head of a creature then folds the top backwards so what he has drawn can't be seen. Then the child passes the paper to the next person who draws the next section of the creature. Then that section is folded over and passed to the next person. When all sections are finished, the group can open the paper to see their collaborative creature!

Crazy Collaborative Creature

February

Puzzle Piece Game

Create two-part puzzle pieces by cutting heart shapes in two. Try to make each cut down the middle slightly different. On Valentine's Day give each student a puzzle piece and they have to find the person that fits their piece and write something nice about them on their piece. Then they children will tape the pieces together and hang them on a bulletin board or around the room. See the pattern below.

Musical Hula Hoops

Gather a half dozen hula hoops or create large circles with yarn on the floor. Put on music and have children dance. When the music stops, each child must get into a circle or hoop. Next take away one hoop and repeat the process. Then take away another hoop or circle each round until all the children try to squeeze into one circle. Silly and fun!

Back to Back Drawing

Pair up your children. Print out or copy the pictures on the next page. Cut the two pictures apart and give one to each pair. Also give the children clipboards with plain white copy paper on them. The children sit in chairs with their backs to each other. To start the game, the first person takes the picture and describes it to their partner. The partner tries to draw the picture. When done, the two children compare the two versions of the picture. Next the partners change positions. Give the second picture to the pair and the other child describes the second picture while the partner draws. When done, they compare the two pictures.

Pictures for Back-to-Back Drawings

1.

2.

March

Reader's Theater

Choose one of the class's favorite books or book chapters and turn it into a play. Have the children create props or pictures of the setting. Assign children to roles in the story and have the children act out the episodes in the book. Teach children how to be a respectful audience and how to clap at the end, and so on.

Once children understand the idea, create groups of 3 or 4 students and have them pick a book and create their own play to share with the rest of the class. You can also find scripts for Reader's Theater online if needed. Give the children time each day for a week to work on their play, then share them all on Friday.

Inside/Outside Circles

Form a circle with half the children in the middle of your group area with children facing out. Then have the rest of the children form another circle outside of them, facing the original group. Give the children one question at a time to discuss with their partner. After each question, the outside group moves one person to the right so everyone has a new partner. Here are possible questions:

- What do you like to do at home?
- What TV shows do you watch?
- What holidays do you celebrate at home? How do you celebrate them?
- What do you like about school?
- What would make school better?
- If you could travel anywhere in the world, where would you go? Why?
- What's your favorite book? Why? Favorite character? Why?
- If you could have a pet, what would you choose? Why?
- Who's your hero? Why?
- What do you think makes a good friend?

We're All Superheroes

For a writing project, have the children create a superhero persona for themselves. Use the template below. During group time, the children can introduce themselves to each other and explain their superpowers. Depending on the grade level, children can also write or dictate a story about their superhero. Put up the children's drawings to make a class bulletin board or class book.

We're All Superheroes!

Name: _____

Superhero Name: _____

My Superhero's Special Power: _____

_____

Here's what my superhero looks like:

April

Partner Obstacle Course

Set up a simple obstacle course outside or in the gym with items such as jumping over a stick, crawling under a chair or table, jumping in a hula hoop, etc. You can also make a path with chalk and mark off areas to jump, squat, turn around, etc.

Match up the children into partners. One child puts a scarf over her eyes so she can't see. The other partner helps her get through the obstacle course. Partners change roles and repeat.

Pat on the Back

Have the children trace one hand on a piece of paper and cut it out. Then the children tape the hand on their back. Classmates mingle and walk around writing something positive on their classmates' hands until everyone has at least 3 positive comments.

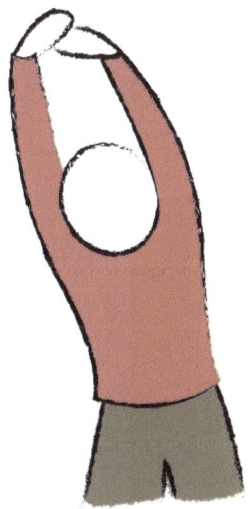

The Wave

Gather the children in a circle. Choose one child to go first. This child makes a stretching movement and the next child repeats it, then the next child, and so on until the "wave" of movement goes completely around the circle. You can repeat this again as many times as you want by having the next child create a new stretching movement to send around the circle.

May

What's Different?

Before the children come back from lunch, or before they enter in the morning, change four or five things in your room, such as moving your desk in a different direction, move a poster to a different wall, add a new visual, switch two children's chairs that are different, etc. When the children return have them try to figure out all the things that are different in the room. The children earn one point for each thing they notice. Do this every day for a week and see how many points they can earn. Award a prize, such as free time, to the entire class.

How Does Your Garden Grow?

Have the children research different plants and flowers that grow in gardens. Next have them choose a plant/flower that they like best and make a picture of that plant/flower. Hang all the flowers up around the room to create your own classroom garden. You can also plant seeds and let the plants grow into a real garden. Point out how special it is when a garden has many different kinds of plants/flowers and how each one is unique!

Parachute Games

Take the children outside and use a parachute together. Emphasize the importance of coordinating the movement and how much you all need to work together. Put a ball inside the parachute and see how high you can get it to bounce up. Call children by name or by attribute (anyone wearing red; children with sneakers; people with curly hair) to run under the parachute when it is up high, then run back out to their spot before it comes down.

June

End of Year Class Book

Have the children write a short reflection on what they remember from this school year (see template below). Then compile these into a class book. If possible, have the children compose their pages in digital form so you can print out a book for each child to take home as a remembrance of the school year in your class.

End of Year Award Ceremony

Hold a special ceremony, inviting families if you can, and create a slide show of photos from throughout the school year. During the ceremony, give an award to every child (See form below) Here are some suggestions:

- Best Reader
- Most Friendly
- Most Athletic
- Best Helper
- Best Artist
- Best in Math
- Best Speller
- Best Singer
- Best Musician
- Most Creative
- Hardest Worker
- Most Cheerful
- Most Improved
- Most Fun
- Most Honest
- Most Kind
- Most Thoughtful
- Hardest Worker
- Best in Homework
- Best Writer
- Best Scientist
- Best Storyteller
- Most Willing to Try New Things
- Best Attendance
- Most Caring
- Most Clever

My School Year

What I liked:

What I learned:

People I will remember:

End-of-Year Read-Aloud Books

The end of the school year brings excitement and often sadness. Celebrations and rituals can help young children prepare for the transition to summer.

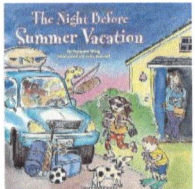 The Night Before Summer Vacation by Natasha Wing. This rhyming book is written in the style of The Night Before Christmas. It's silly, fun, and the children can chime in on the ends of the lines with rhymes.

 No More Pencils, No More Books, No More Teacher's Dirty Looks by Diane deGroat. This 1st grade boy worries about getting an award at the end of the year. The happy ending includes excitement about the end-of-year festivities.

 Last Day Blues by Julie Danneberg. On the last day of school, the children come up with a gift for their teaching that shows her all the things they'll miss about school. Charming!

 The Last Day of Kindergarten by Nancy Loewen. This kindergarten girl is sad that the school year is ending but realizes it's also exciting to be starting a new grade soon.

 The Last Day of School by Louise Borden. At the end of the school year, a 3rd grade boy tries to decide when to give his teacher his special gift. This is a longer book that's perfect for upper elementary grades.

 Miss Bindergarten Celebrates the Last Day of Kindergarten by Joseph Slate. In this alphabet book, the kindergartners celebrate the last day of kindergarten in humorous ways.

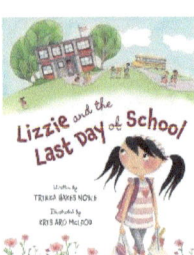 Lizzie and the Last Day of School by Trinka Hakes Noble. This is a good book for children who love everything about school and don't really want it to be over.

 Last Day Hooray! by Nancy Poydar. In Mrs. Bell's class, the children are all dreaming about what they will do during the summer as they happily prepare for the end of the school year.

Part 3: Developing School Success Skills

Developing School Success Skills Overview

Being successful in school takes more than just being smart. Children need to also get along with others, be able to focus, calm themselves down, and control their bodies. We know that most children who misbehave are lacking social and emotional skills. Perhaps they never learned them at home. Perhaps they just have a more difficult time learning them, such as children on the autism spectrum or children with learning disabilities. In order to prevent misbehaviors in your classroom, you need to systematically teach the social and emotional skills that children need to be successful in school.

In order to build a classroom community, all the children in your class need the social and emotional skills required for learning together for many hours a day. In The Positive Classroom Method, you will implement a social/emotional skills curriculum by focusing on one skill per week for the first month, then one skill per month for the rest of the school year.

If you find that the children in your class need a particular skill in order to be successful, feel free to move around the various skills. For example, if you have children who have a lot of trouble keeping their bodies still, move that skill earlier in the year. If you have children who are particularly kind and don't tattle, you can skip that skill.

The next page provides an overview of the curriculum for the whole year. Print this out to keep in your plan book so you remember which skills to work on. Throughout the year, you can repeat many of these activities over and over again. Children need *many* repetitions of these activities to learn them well enough to use them on their own.

School Success Skills Curriculum for the Year

Date	Social/Emotional Skill Unit
September	Greetings & Manners
September	Saying Kind Words
September	Calming Down
September	Tattling vs. Telling
October	Conflict Resolution
November	Staying Focused and Building Stamina
December	Sharing & Working Together
January	Identifying, Labeling, and Expressing Feelings
February	Being a Good Friend
March	Keeping My Body Still
April	Grit: How to Keep Going When Things Are Hard
May	Self-Monitoring and Evaluation

September Week 1: Greetings and Manners

The best way to start building a community in your classroom is to teach children greetings and manners. No matter what age the students are, they will benefit from a shared understanding of classroom behaviors. Since children will have learned all kinds of different behaviors at home, it's important to start off the year with developing your own classroom culture.

Teaching Manners

1. Decide what greetings and manners you want children to use in your classroom. Here are some suggestions:
- When to say "Please" and "Thank You"
- When to say "Excuse me" and "I'm Sorry"
- Saying "good morning" with eye contact, smile, handshake
- Not interrupting
- How to get someone's attention
- Using appropriate language/Curse words
- Saying kind words
- Never making fun of anyone, pointing, teasing, etc.
- Sneezing/ having good hygiene, avoiding spreading germs
- Holding door for others
- How to act when a guest enters classroom

You can teach the first four of these as Magic Words since they are used so often.

2. Teach each manner in a whole group lesson by explaining and modeling the behavior. Have some children also demonstrate and role play situations. Have all children turn to a partner and practice. See the lesson plans below.

3. Praise children when they use manners properly. Have a "Manner of the Day." Let the children know that you will be looking for how they use that manner during the day. Then, be sure to praise the child each time you see or hear that manner being used.

4. Model these manners yourself.

5. Review and remind children of these manners frequently throughout the year.

Please and Thank You Lesson Plans

Objective: For children to be able to recognize when to say please and thank you.

Materials: Stick to use as a "Magic Wand"
Individual White Boards
Chart Paper or SmartBoard
"Please" and "Thank You" Signs and Lanyard

Procedure:

1. Gather children together and explain that there are magic words we use in school. Have them write down what words they think are magic words (or have them turn to a partner and tell them what they think are magic words). Tell them that they are "magic" words because they make us feel better and they make the class a happier place.

2. Ask for the children's suggestions and write them on the chart paper or SmartBoard. Explain that today you will focus on saying "Please" and "Thank You."

3. Ask for a volunteer to come up and role play with you. Act out some of the following scenarios (see the cards below):

- You drop your pencil. A classmate picks it up and gives it to you. You say, "Thank you."
- Your friend is playing with something you want. You say, "Please, can I have a turn?"
- A classmate helps you open your lunch container. You say, "Thank you."
- The teacher tells you that she likes your new sneakers. You say, "Thank you."
- A classmate asks if you want to work with her. You say, "Yes, please."
- The teacher asks if you'd like milk with lunch. You say, "Yes, please." When she gives it to you, you say, "Thank you."

Use the signs on the next few pages during your role play. The children can give a choral response when you hold up the sign, or you can give each child a copy to hold up. You can also post these signs so that the children remember their importance.

4. During the day, whenever you hear someone say, "Please" or "Thank You," be sure to point it out. For example, "I've heard a lot of people saying Thank You today." or "I noticed that Mark and Jennifer both said Thank You to their partners. That's a good use of manners!"

5. Reminders (see the following pages): If you have a couple of children who are having trouble with Please and Thank You, make a small sign that they can keep on their desks to remind them. You can also create a Please and Thank You Lanyard that you wear around your neck. Just hold up the apporiate side to cue the children.

"Thank you!"

Thank You!

Please and Thank You Reminder Lanyard

"Please"

"Thank You"

Cards for Please and Thank You Role Play

You drop your pencil. A classmate picks it up and gives it to you. You say, "Thank you."	Your friend is playing with something you want. You say, "Please, can I have a turn?"
A classmate helps you open your lunch container. You say, "Thank you."	The teacher tells you that she likes your new sneakers. You say, "Thank You."
A classmate asks if you want to work with her. You say, "Yes, please."	The teacher asks if you'd like milk with lunch. You say, "Yes, please." When she gives it to you, you say, "Thank you."
The classmate who sits next to you starts talking while you are trying to work. You say, "Can you please stop talking so I can work? Thank you."	You sit at the art table with another child. You'd like the can of markers that is over on their side of the table. You say, "Can you please pass me the markers?"

"Excuse Me" and "I'm Sorry" Lesson Plan

Objective: Children will be able to say, "Excuse Me" and "I'm Sorry" at appropriate times.

Materials: Scenario Cards; Manners Cards; Magic Words Sign

Procedures: Gather the children on the carpet and tell them you are going to play a manners game. Today we will focus on saying two more sets of magic words: "Excuse Me" and "I'm Sorry." Let's play a game.

> **Thumbs Up or Thumbs Down:** PreK- 1st grade:
> Have a child come up to the front of the circle to act out one of the scenarios on the following page. The rest of the children should judge whether the child said the right thing or not. If they agree, they put a thumbs up or if they think it was wrong, a thumbs down. If the card is a thumbs down, ask the children what they should say instead.
>
> **Find a Partner Game** (2nd- 5th grade)
> Cut out the **Manners Cards** on the following pages. Give each child one card. Some will have cards with scenarios on them and some will have cards with "Excuse Me" or "I'm Sorry." On your signal, have the children find a person whose card matches theirs. Mix up the cards and play again.

Throughout the week, after you've played the game once or twice, notice any child who is using these manners correctly. Be sure to offer praise and positive feedback.

Post the *Magic Words* sign and refer to it as needed to help the children develop good habits. These must be practiced over and over again until they become second nature for the children.

"Excuse Me" and "I'm Sorry" Scenario Cards for Thumbs Up and Thumbs Down Game

Lots of kids are getting their coats to go home so it's crowded. You want to squeeze in to get your coat. You say, "Get out of my way!"	You are trying to line up but a couple of kids are in the way. You say, "Excuse me."
You are getting ready to sit down on the carpet for group time. You accidently bump into one of your classmates. You say, "I'm sorry."	You borrow a friend's pencil and you forget to return it. The next day you realize it and you give it back. You say, "I'm sorry."
The teacher is talking to another adult. You tap her on the leg and say, "Teacher, teacher!"	You walk past the table where a classmate is eating breakfast. You knock into her arm by mistake and her milk spills. You say, "I'm sorry!"
You are trying to get into line to go outside. You move too fast and you knock into the kid next to you. You say, "I'm sorry. Are you okay?"	The class is writing in their journals. You forgot to get a pencil but your neighbor has a couple of them on his desk. You just grab one to use.
Your friend tells you his mom is home sick. You say, "I'm sorry. I hope she feels better soon."	You want to sit at one of the tables for snack. Your classmate has her lunch things all over the place. You say, "Excuse me, could you move your things over a little bit?

The Positive Classroom ©thepositiveclassroom.org

Manners Cards

Excuse Me	I'm Sorry	I'm Sorry
Excuse Me	I'm Sorry	I'm Sorry
Excuse Me	I'm Sorry	I'm Sorry
Excuse Me	Excuse Me	I'm Sorry
Excuse Me	Excuse Me	I'm Sorry
Excuse Me	Excuse Me	I'm Sorry

Manners Cards

You are in a hurry and you bump into a classmate on your way into the classroom. You say, _____	You are trying to sit at the table but there isn't a lot of room. You squeeze in, saying, _____	You knock into a classmate and she drops her books. You say _____ and help her pick them up.
It's quiet reading time and your neighbor starts chatting with you. You say _____. I need to work.	Your teacher is talking to another student. You wait until she stops talking and then you say, _____	You accidently tear a page in your math book. You go get some tape to fix it and you say, _____
You said something mean to a classmate and you realize that you shouldn't have. You say, _____	You are walking in the hallway and you're not paying attention so you bump into your classmate. You say, _____	At snack, you knock over your juice box and it spills on your classmate's sleeve. You say _____ and help clean it up.
On the playground you throw a ball that hits someone. You check that they are okay and say, _____	You pick up someone's pencil by mistake, thinking it was yours. They ask for it back. You say, _____	Two kids are standing by the door and you want to get by to go to the bathroom. You say, _____
The teacher asks you a question, but you didn't hear her. You say, _____	You need to reach in front of your classmate to get a marker on the desk. You say, _____	The teacher is writing on the board during seatwork. You want to ask to go to the bathroom. You say, _____

September, Week 2: Saying Kind Words

Many children are not exposed to people saying kind words and they need to learn a repertoire of kind things they can say. This skill is very important to teach early in the school year because it helps with building community.

Objective: Children will say kind words to their classmates at appropriate times.

Materials: Chart Paper

Procedures:

1. Gather the children together. Describe for them a classroom that is really wonderful, where everyone is nice to each other and gets along. Tell them that we can all have this classroom if we learn to be kind to others. One of the best ways to be kind is to say kind words.

Ask the children to generate a list of kind things they can say to each other. Write the list on chart paper.

2. Tell the children that you will be listening throughout the day for kind words.

3. Post the chart where the children can see it. Throughout the day, point to the chart and remind the children about their kind words.

4. Be sure to praise children whenever you hear them say kind words.

5. At the end of the day, gather the children and review the kind words. Ask the children to remember any times that they heard the kind words.

6. Every morning for at least a week, review the kind words. After that, review the kind words chart once a week.

September Week 3: Calming Down

Choose one or more of the following strategies to teach the whole class. Children need to practice these skills over and over again when they are calm so that they can use them when they are upset. Pick a time of day to review them – perhaps during morning meeting and again after lunch. You can also use these any time the class has too much energy, such as after specials or going outside. During the day, individual children will need to be reminded to use the skills until they become second nature.

Flower and Candle Breathing

Gather the children on the carpet. Model for them how to breathe in deeply while pretending to sniff a flower by holding up their closed fist. Then very slowly exhale, pretending to blow out a candle. It's important to teach children to exhale slowly and gently.

Three in and three out

Get the children in a relaxed position, then have them close their eyes and breathe in as you count "one." Then, without breathing out, have them breathe in a bit deeper as you count to "two," then once more have them fully fill their lungs as you count "three." The exhale works the same way. You say, "Okay, one, now exhale a little bit," Next you say, "Two, blow out a little more," and then, "Three, let out the rest of your breath." This works best if you model this first a few times and have them do it with you before starting to close their eyes. They can also pretend to gradually blow up a balloon with each breath and then let the air out slowly.

Think of a Happy Place

Have the children close their eyes and imagine themselves in a calm, happy place where they feel warm and safe. Tell them that they can go back to this place and feel good by closing their eyes and bringing this image into their mind. As children get tired or cranky throughout the day, you can remind them to close their eyes for a moment and go back to their happy place.

Yoga Poses

Yoga can help children gain body awareness and self-control of their bodies, which is an important step in self-regulation. The following are some possible poses to use with young children. Have the children pay attention to their breathing while in the poses. Have fun with these and encourage children to create their own poses, too!

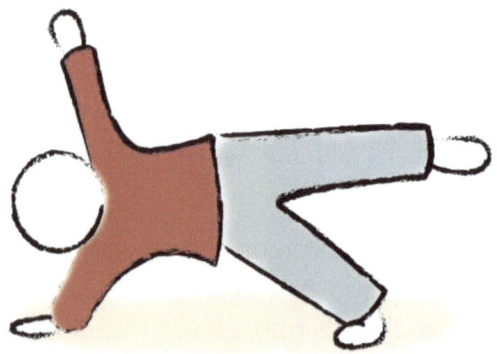

Mountain

This is a good pose to start with. Show the children a picture of a mountain and have them imagine how straight, tall and steady they can be while standing still. Hold shoulders slightly back and feet flat on the floor.

Cat/Dog

Children get down on hands and knees. Arms should be right under the shoulders with their back flat. They gently arch their back up high like a cat as they breathe out. Then as they breathe in, they let their back sag down like a dog. Gently alternate between the two for a few more breaths.

Tree

Children stand on one leg with the opposite foot resting against their ankle or calf. After they've gained their balance, they gently raise their arms like a tree as they exhale. Hold the "branches" up in the air for a few more breaths.

I will take 5 deep breaths

| 1 | 2 | 3 | 4 | 5 |

Small Cards for I Will Take 5 Deep Breaths Card

Cut out and laminate these cards. Put Velcro on the back. Laminate the "I Will Take 5 Deep Breaths Card" and put Velcro on the white squares. Teach the child to put on one picture for each deep breath. Store the cards in a Ziploc bag all together. Keep the Breath Cards in your Calm-Down Kit.

Week 4: Tattling vs. Telling

Some children get into the habit of tattling as a way of getting attention. You can easily prevent this or get it to stop by teaching the children the difference between tattling and telling. Be sure that you have also taught the children to say kind words and that you are giving a lot of positive attention to kind words. Try to give as little attention to tattling as possible. Also teach Conflict Resolution (see plans for October) if children need help resolving their conflicts.

Teach "Tattling vs. Telling"

Objective: Children will be able to distinguish tattling in order to get someone in trouble and telling in order to help someone in trouble.

Materials: Tattling vs. Telling Poster and Worksheet

Procedure:

1. Ask the children to tell you what tattling is and why someone might tattle.

2. Explain that in your classroom, we are always kind, so we need to find better solutions than tattling. Show the poster of Tattling vs. Telling and explain the difference between the two actions. Have two children role play.

3. Practice with Scenarios:
>Younger children: Read the scenarios on the Tattling vs. Telling Worksheet and have them put a thumbs up if it's telling and a thumbs down if it is tattling.
>
>Older children: Pass out the worksheet and have children complete it. If they finish early, they can write down additional scenarios that they remember.

4. Hang up the poster. If you find that children are tattling, you can point to the poster and ask them, "Are you tattling or telling?"

5. You may need to repeat this lesson again, or at least remind the children for a few weeks about Tattling vs. Telling during your morning meeting.

Tattling or Telling?

Tattling: Hurts Someone

Telling: Helps Someone

Tattling or Telling?

Read the description. Circle whether the child is tattling or telling:

1. Marisa complains to the teacher that Michael took her pencil.	Tattling	Telling
2. Jessica lets the teacher know that Jamal fell and hurt his knee.	Tattling	Telling
3. Vanessa tells that teacher that Rachel bothered her in aftercare yesterday.	Tattling	Telling
4. Alex says that Andre is bothering him while he's trying to work.	Tattling	Telling
5. Megan lets the teacher know that Jasmine needs help in the bathroom.	Tattling	Telling
6. Kyle complains that Sam said a bad word.	Tattling	Telling
7. Jessica gets the teacher and tell her that Lilly is crying.	Tattling	Telling
8. Denise says that Luke won't leave her alone.	Tattling	Telling
9. Matthew whines that Justin cuts the line.	Tattling	Telling
10. Jon tells the teacher that Frankie is bleeding and needs a Band-Aid.	Tattling	Telling

October: Conflict Resolution

Conflict resolution is a *learned* skill. Children need to learn to identify other children's emotions, and specific strategies for resolving conflicts. This month, you can directly teach some of these strategies, then the remainder of the year, you should model conflict resolution again and again until the children begin to handle this on their own.

Modeling How to Solve Conflicts in Everyday Interactions

The following steps (from Epstein, 2009) should be used to model for children how to solve problems. These are best taught when there is an actual conflict.

1. Establish safety

Approach the situation calmly and stop any actions that could hurt someone. Your ability to stay calm and collected is very important in modeling social skills for the children and for being able to think clearly yourself.

> For example, first-graders Dylan and Matthew are arguing during center time. Matthew is grabbing a game that is in Dylan's hands. You gently put your arm on Matthew's shoulder and separate the two boys.

2. Acknowledge the children's feelings

Describing the child's feelings helps the children to be able to listen to you, identify his feelings, and learn how feelings lead to behaviors and consequences.

> "Matthew, I can tell you are very angry right now. And Dylan, you seem to be scared that Matthew will hurt you." As children get better at this process, you should ask the children to interpret each other's feelings: "Matthew, how do you think Dylan is feeling right now?" "Dylan, how do you think Matthew is feeling?"

3. Gather information

Allow the children to explain their view points, even if you observed the actions. Do not take sides. You will be modeling for the children how to think through problems.

> "Dylan, can you tell me what happened?" Dylan begins and Matthew interrupts. "Matthew, as soon as he is done, you can tell me what happened, too." Dylan says

that Matthew tried to take the game he was using and he had it first. "Okay, Matthew, it's your turn to tell us what happened." Matthew says, "I really want to play with that. I didn't get a turn in forever. And Dylan won't share with me."

4. Restate the problem

Describe the problem without judgment. Do not use terms like inconsiderate, selfish, or stubborn. Just describe what happened. This allows the children to know that they have been heard and understood, and it helps them to see the problem more clearly.

"So, it sounds like Dylan was playing with this game and Matthew really wanted a turn with it. Dylan was not ready to share, and Matthew tried to take the game so he could have a turn."

5. Ask for solutions

Try to get the children to generate possible solutions rather than just pronouncing a solution yourself. If the children come up with the ideas themselves, they are more likely to follow them, and eventually to learn how to do this on their own. In the beginning, children might need a lot of help in order to generate solutions.

"Matthew and Dylan, do you have any suggestions for how we can solve this problem?" Dylan says, "He should leave me alone. I had it first." "Okay, is that a good idea or not?" Matthew chimes in, "No, I want a turn too. How about I get a turn in five minutes?" "That's one idea. Any others?" Dylan suggests, "We could play the game together." "Okay, that's another idea. Which idea do you want to try?" Matthew says, "Okay, let's play it together. But I get the game first tomorrow." "How does that sound, Dylan?" "Okay."

6. Provide follow-up support

After a problem-solving choice is made, check back with the children to be sure the solution is being followed and is working. Give positive feedback to let them know how well they've worked at problem solving.

"Matthew and Dylan, how is your solution working?" "Okay. Jesse wanted to play, too, so we're all gonna play it now." "Great thinking. You did a terrific job of solving this problem." In your feedback, focus on the good job they did with the process, rather than the good idea itself. We want to teach children that the process is the important thing to focus on.

Epstein, A. (2009). Resolving conflict. In A. Epstein (Ed.). *Me, you, us: Social-emotional learning in pre-school* (pp. 111– 124). Ypsilanti, MI: High Scope Press

Practicing Problem Solving

Objective: Children will be able to follow the five steps in solving problems

Materials: Conflict Resolution Poster; Conflict scenarios

Procedures:

1. Introduction: Start by eliciting what the children know about conflict. Make a concept web on the board or chart paper with "CONFLICT" in the circle in the middle. Discuss these ideas. Next, tell a story about two children who were fighting or arguing. This is best if you can recall a recent example from your classroom.

2. Explanation: Go over the five steps on the Conflict Resolution Poster. Use the following scenario and have two children act out the situation:

> John: Jeremy was pushing me!
>
> Jeremy: He was trying to cut the line!
>
> Teacher: Let's look at the conflict resolution steps. The first thing is to stop and breathe. Okay, good. Now let's do Step 2: Listen to each other. Jeremy, you go first.
>
> Jeremy: John, you were trying to cut the line. I was there first.
>
> John: I want to be first. You always get there first and I want a turn.
>
> Teacher: You did a good job of listening to each other. Now, what do you think the problem is?
>
> Jeremy: We both want to be first in line.
>
> Teacher: Okay, now what solutions can you both come up with?
>
> John: Don't run to get in line when the bell rings?
>
> Jeremy: Don't get upset if you're not first in line?
>
> John: Say, "Excuse me" when you want to get past someone?
>
> Jeremy: How about using Rock, Paper, Scissors to decide who's first?
>
> Teacher: Great ideas! I'm impressed. Which one do you want to try?
>
> John: How about Rock, Paper, Scissors?
>
> Jeremy: Yeah, that sounds good!

3. Practice: See if the children have any comments or questions. Practice this with more scenarios over the next few days. Hang the Conflict Resolution Poster where the children can refer to it. If you see children arguing, remind them to follow the steps.

Conflict Resolution Scenarios:

Maria is upset because Jenny said she can't come to her birthday party.	Jillian took Julissa's markers off of her desk because she couldn't find her own. When Julissa saw her with the markers, she yelled at her and grabbed them back.
Keisha and Alex are working as partners during Math centers and they are arguing about how to share the pattern blocks. Alex says that Keisha took too many.	Kareem is reading quietly during Readers' Workshop. Rebecca is sitting close to him and keeps interrupting him to chat. Kareem gets really angry and pushes Rebecca away.
Eric bumped into Jared when he was getting his coat. Jared got really mad and pushed Eric out of the way and yelled at him.	Emma and Olivia both race to be the first ones to use the new computers. They begin to argue.

Conflict Resolution

1. Stop & Breathe

2. Listen to each other

3. State the problem

4. Think of solutions

5. Try out one solution

What to Do When Someone Bothers You
(How to say "NO" appropriately)

Objective: Children will be able to respond politely and appropriately when someone is bothering them.

Materials: Chart paper, role play cards

Procedures:

1. Gather children together and have them brainstorm ways that other people might bother them. Write these on chart paper.

2. Next role play how children could respond appropriately when someone is bothering them. Use the scenario cards on the next page for examples. Teach the children to say, "Please stop that" or "I don't like that" or "Please leave me alone." Teach them that they can move away, or ask a teacher for help.

3. Ask the children what they noticed about how you responded.

4. Have a couple of children role play how they would respond. Ask the children what they noticed.

5. Pair up the children and give them each a role play card. Have them act out the scenario for practice. Praise children who respond appropriately.

Repeat this lesson 2 or 3 more times during the month. Be sure to point out and praise when you hear children using the phrases they have learned.

Scenario Cards for What to Do When Someone Bothers You

You are lined up waiting to go to lunch. The person in front of you keeps bumping into you. What can you do? What can you say?	You are trying to read quietly to yourself. Another child sits down right next to you and it makes it hard for you to pay attention to your book. What can you do? What can you say?
You are writing in your journal but one of the kids who sits close to you is talking and bothering you. What can you do? What can you say?	Your friend comes to school angry and he starts to pick a fight with you. What can you do? What can you say?
During math, your partner grabs all the pattern blocks. What can you do? What can you say?	You are sharing a computer with your partner in order to do research. She won't let you see the screen. What can you do? What can you say?
You're on the playground and some of the kids are teasing you. What can you do? What can you say?	The kid sitting behind you keeps poking you with a pencil. What can you do? What can you say?
You are trying to hang up your coat and it is crowded. The other children are pushing you. What can you do? What can you say?	You are sitting on the carpet for morning meeting. One of the children is sitting too close to you. What can you do? What can you say?

Conflict Resolution Read-Alouds

Here are some suggested titles to generate discussions. You can use your language arts strategies and integrate them into your social skills training, such as making predictions, identifying the main idea, or describing characters' feelings.

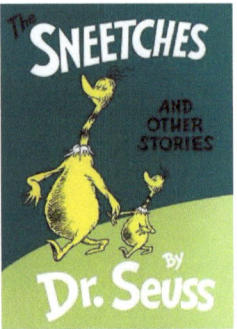 The Sneetches and Other Stories – Dr. Suess. This book provides an opportunity to discuss social categories with primary grade (and older) children.

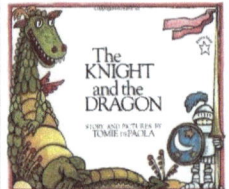 The Knight and the Dragon – Tomie DePaola. What happens when the Knight and Dragon are not good at fighting? This book with few words allows for plenty of discussion.

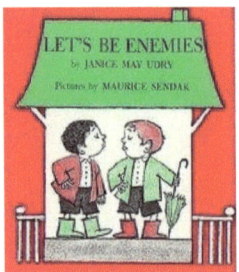 Lets Be Enemies – Janice May Udry. What happens when best friends don't get along? Pre-K to 2nd grade will be able to relate to this book.

 Enemy Pie – Derek Munson. A clever story about what happens when enemies have to spend a day together. Appropriate for grades 1-3.

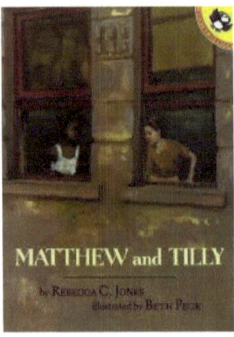 Matthew and Tilly – Rebecca C. Jones. Primary grade children will learn about the themes of friendships and quarreling from this book.

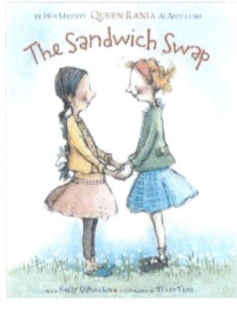 The Sandwich Shop - Queen Rania of Jordan Al Abdullah. The theme of this book is that friendship is more powerful than difference. Grades K-2.

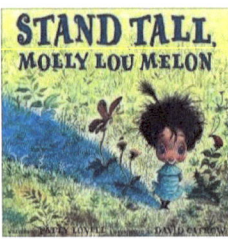 Stand Tall, Molly Lou Melon – Patty Lovell An unusual girl handles bullying in this book for grades K-3.

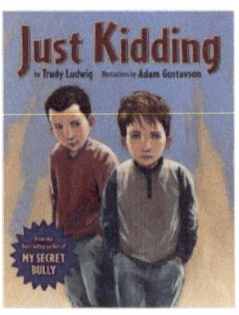 Just Kidding – Trudy Ludwig. This realistic portrayal of boys bullying is appropriate for grades 2-5.

November: How to Stay Focused and Build Stamina

Many teachers assume that children are just not trying hard enough to pay attention or they are not held accountable for their actions and need to be pushed harder. They are missing the possibility that these children don't know *how* to pay attention.

Some children (and adults) do not have the skills to maintain focus. This is part of what psychologists call "Executive Function" and it involves the pre-frontal cortex of the brain. When this skill is underdeveloped, it makes it hard for children to control their impulses, maintain focus, and hold information in their working memory. It's not really the case that the child can't pay attention – it's that they can't pay attention to what you want them to pay attention to. Many children, especially those with ADHD, pay attention to everything happening around them, and can't selectively focus on one thing. The good news is that paying attention can be taught.

In order to help children learn to focus and build their stamina, you need to treat this as a skill that must be learned and practiced – just like learning the alphabet or how to multiply. On the next few pages are some lesson plans for helping children learn to pay attention and stay on task for longer and longer periods of time.

How to Stay Focused: Tracking the Speaker

Tracking means that children keep their eyes on the speaker. This means looking at the teacher or other children when they are speaking. Do not allow children to look at their papers, or play with items in their desk, or look around the room. They should turn their bodies, if needed, to follow the speaker.

Objective: Children will be able to keep their eyes on the speaker and turn their body as needed.

Materials: None needed

Procedure:

1. Explain why tracking is important. (To help you focus, listen, and pay attention.)

2. Model how to track the speaker. Be sure to use Learner's Position that you taught as a procedure.

3. Ask the children what they noticed.

4. Have a couple of children model how to track the speaker.

5. Ask the children what they noticed.

6. Have everyone practice. Praise the children who do it correctly.

Practice:

During your lessons for the rest of the day, be sure to remind children to track the speaker and praise those who do it correctly. Do not allow children to look around the room, play with items in their desk, look at their papers, and so on. Insist gently that all children continue to track. Require 100% compliance on this. If you forget or get lazy about reminding them, they will develop bad habits. Do this until it becomes second nature. For the rest of the school year, be sure to continue to remind children and praise them.

Track the Speaker

How to Stay Focused: Mindfulness Practice

Research is showing that mindfulness exercises can calm the class and improve academic achievement. It can also help children with attention problems learn to focus better. The best exercise is to simply spend about 2 minutes in quiet stillness. This can be done daily in the morning, after lunch, or in the middle of an activity when children start to lose focus.

Objective: Children will be able to sit quietly without talking and focus on their breathing for at least two minutes.

Materials: Chime or Bell.

Procedures:

1. Explain to children that mindfulness is a wonderful way to calm down and learn to focus.

2. Model for children how to sit quietly. Ring the chime, then close your eyes and slowly breathe in and out.

3. Ask the children what they noticed.

4. Have everyone practice:
   - If children are on the carpet, have them sit cross-legged. If they are at desks or tables, have them put their feet on the floor and hands in their lap.
   - Ring the chime.
   - Children should close their eyes.
   - Prompt them to breathe in slowly and breathe out slowly.
   - Remind them to notice how they are breathing.
   - After a minute or two, ring the chime and invite children to slowly open their eyes.
   - As children get good at this, increase the time to 3-4 minutes.
   - Children might giggle and laugh in the beginning, but if you show that you are serious, they will follow suit. Be confident and gentle.

How to Stay Focused: Self-Monitoring

Children need to learn to monitor whether they are paying attention or not. Visual aids can help. Tape a picture of a child working (either listening to the teacher or working on seatwork) and write: "Am I Focused?" on it as a reminder. See example below. Cut this out and give each child (or those who need it) a copy to keep on their desk.

Timers

When used as a self-monitoring device, timers can help children gain some self-control. They can be used to help a child stay focused and take a break, as described above, or they can be set for smaller increments, say 30 seconds or a minute, to help children self-monitor. When the timer goes off, the children can check whether or not they are paying attention.

Building Stamina

As children learn ways to improve their focus, they should also start to develop their stamina. This means being able to stay on task for longer and longer periods of time. I recommend you teach children stamina first with getting them to read to themselves.

Objective: Children will build stamina and be able to read to themselves for longer and longer periods of time.

Materials: Stamina Chart (see below) and independent reading books for each child.

Procedures:

1. Create a behavior chart with the children's input that describes what children should be doing during reading time. Highlight the following:
   - Stay in one spot
   - Get started right away
   - Read the whole time
   - Read quietly or whisper read

2. Have a child model how to do this and ask the children what they notice. Have another child model the wrong way and ask the children what they notice. Have the same child then model the right way again. Next have all the children practice these behaviors.

3. Tell the children that today they are going to start building stamina. Compare this to learning to be a good runner and how runners start out with shorter amounts and gradually run farther and farther.

4. Send the children to their reading spots and let them get started. Watch the group carefully and when you see any of the children lose focus, stop the reading time and bring them back to the whole group area.

5. Show them the stamina chart and fill in the amount of time they were all able to read. Don't be surprised if it's only a minute or two to start out. Congratulate the children on their success and suggest that tomorrow perhaps they can go longer. Keep the chart going for the next few weeks or so until this becomes easier.

STAMINA CHART
SUBJECT:_____

minutes

day — m t w th f m t w th f m t w th f m t w th f

December: Sharing & Working Together

Even adults have trouble sharing and taking turns, so this is a skill that needs to be taught and practiced regularly in school. We often assume that children understand what they are supposed to do when we ask them to share or take turns, but they usually need to know exactly what we expect.

Three Ways to Share

Objective: Children will be able to demonstrate three ways to share materials.

Materials: Any materials that children will need to share in your classroom, such as math manipulatives, markers, books, and so on.

Procedures:

1. Ask the children to turn to their "Turn and Talk" partner and discuss what it means to share. Then ask them to come up with ways to share math materials (or whatever else you are using). Write down their ideas on chart paper.

2. Summarize their ideas into three categories and show them the poster about sharing.

A. Half & Half: One person uses half, the other person uses half, or each person does a different task.
- One child gets half the pattern blocks and the other child gets half.
- Two children are making a poster. One child colors one side, the other child colors the other side.
- The children are making sculptures from toothpicks and marshmallows. Each child at the table gets a handful of marshmallows and toothpicks and they make their own sculpture.

B. You Go, I Go: One person uses the materials for a time period; then the other person gets a turn.
- One person uses the green marker, then the other person gets a turn to use it.
- One child uses the computer while the other child writes, then they switch.
- One child uses the magnifying glass, then she passes it to the next child.

C. Two Together: Both persons use the materials together.
- The two children put the book in between them and they both read it together.
- Three children are playing a card game. They all have cards and play together.
- The table has a bin of markers. They stay in the middle and everyone uses them.

3. Give each pair of children another set of materials and have them practice the three ways to share.

4. Hang up the **Three Ways to Share** poster and refer to it whenever you ask the children to work together. Different types of sharing work better for different kinds of materials so before you start an activity, have the children demonstrate appropriate ways they might share.

How to Help a Friend with School Work

Model for the children how to help someone with their seatwork or when they are partner reading. Often children jump right in and give them the answer or read the word. Explain and model how to give wait time, and how to give hints instead of just telling them how to do it.

Working in Teams

There are lots of advantages to having children work in teams or groups, however, they need to be taught exactly how to collaborate. Use the GROUPS poster below to start a conversation about how to work together:

G	Get along. Say kind words.
R	Respect others' ideas. Listen.
O	Offer help to your team-mates.
U	Use a quiet voice.
P	Participate fully. Everyone does the work.
S	Stay on task. Build stamina.

Have children model the best way to work together. Discuss what might go wrong. If you are working with younger children, teach them to work together in pairs first. Then, once they can do this smoothly, put two pairs together to create groups of 4.

Three Ways to Share

1. Half and Half
2. You Go, I Go
3. Two Together

Working in Groups

Get along. Say kind words.

Respect others' ideas. Listen.

Offer help to team-mates.

Use a quiet voice.

Participate. Everyone works.

Stay on Task. Build stamina.

January: Identifying, Labeling, and Expressing Feelings

At the heart of social-emotional competence is the ability to identify, label and express feelings. This month, focus on the following activities. In addition to whole-group lessons, there are many "teachable moments" when working with feelings.

Emotion Photos

Have the children practice making an emotional expression with their face or body. Then take a photo of each child. Print these out and have the children cut them out and paste them on index cards. Show the children the list of emotion words and have them label the photo. Post these around the room or use them for other activities.

Emotion Thermometer

Print the thermometer poster to and hang it up in your classroom. During a whole-group mini-lesson, demonstrate how to use the thermometer. You can print a copy for each child and then pair the children up. Have each partner talk about where they are on the thermometer right at that moment and then what it feels like to be at different levels on the thermometer. Don't use this when children are upset, but rather use it to check in with children during your morning Meet and Greet or other times during the day. This helps them learn to recognize their own emotional state, which is the first step in emotional regulation.

Emotions Partner Game

Brainstorm with the children a list of emotion words. Write these on chart paper. Next, pair up the children. Have one child use their body or face to show an emotion. The other child tries to guess the type of emotion. Then switch. This can be used as a quick Brain Break throughout the month.

Writing about Emotions

During your narrative writing lessons, assign the children to add emotion words to their writing. Have a list of emotion words for them to refer to (use the one below or create your own).

Label Emotions during the Day

Throughout the normal events of the day, and when conflicts occur, it is helpful to label children's emotions for them so that they begin to distinguish between different emotions and know what specific emotions feel like.

For example, when A'isha comes into the classroom and slams her backpack down on the desk and scowls, you might say, "Hi A'isha. It looks like you are very angry this morning. Can you tell me about it?"

Or imagine that Mariah has just bumped into Robert as she tries to sit down for group reading time on the carpet. Robert blows up and tries to push her away. You could intervene and use this as an opportunity to label emotions while still helping children learn more appropriate responses: "Robert, it looks like you are angry that Mariah bumped into you. I can understand that, but I can't let you hurt Mariah. Does anyone have some suggestions for what we can do when we are angry at someone that won't hurt them?" You can then elicit suggestions that might include telling the other person how you feel, for example.

Labeling Story Emotions

During your read-alouds or guided reading, give the children a copy of the handout on the next page with emotional faces. Stop at appropriate times during the story and have the children point to the face that they think best describes the emotion of the story at that point.

How Do You Feel Today?

Feeling Words

Annoyed

Tearful

Joyous

ANGRY

Ashamed

CALM

Frightened

Surprised

Happy

MISERABLE

SAD

Glad

Bored

Hurt

Depressed

Worried

CONFUSED

How am I feeling?

Read-Alouds that Focus on Feelings

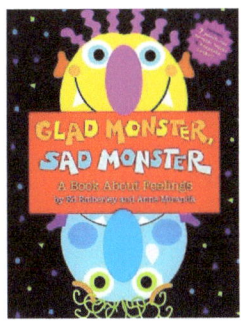

Glad Monster, Sad Monster: A Book About Emotions - Ed Emberley & Anne Miranda. This book includes die-cut masks of monsters showing different feelings and is good for teaching emotional vocabulary. The colorful, creative illustrations will be enjoyed by children in preschool – 1st grade.

The Rainbow Fish – Marcus Pfister. This award-winning book focuses on a beautiful fish who is sad and rejected. He learns to share and gains acceptance and friendship. This book provides primary school children with opportunities to discuss the characters' feelings.

Today I Feel Silly: And Other Moods That Make My Day – Jamie Lee Curtis. This rhyming book presents a girl expressing a different feeling each day. This is a good discussion-starter and vocabulary-builder for children in grades K-2.

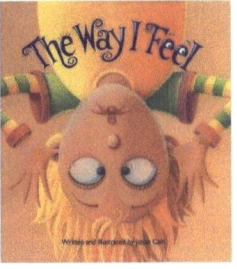

The Way I feel – Janan Cain. This is another book with bright illustrations that depict a variety of feelings, including silly, bored, angry, sad, scared, shy, jealous. Preschool and kindergarten children will enjoy this book while learning how to identify their own feelings.

The Lemonade War – Jacqueline Davies. Evan and Jesse are competing to make money in their lemonade stands. Children in grades 3-5 will relate to the emotions expressed by the characters in this book. Studying the character development can lead to discussion about identifying and expressing emotions.

February: How to Be a Good Friend

In order for children to get their needs met for love and attention, peer friendships are very important. The more comfortable children feel at school, the more ready they are to learn. Being accepted and feeling a part of the group is a big part of feeling comfortable. Many children who constantly seek attention and misbehave throughout the day are lacking basic skills in peer relationships. It is worth it to teach all of the class some of these basic skills.

How to Be Kind

Gather the children and ask them to turn to their partner and talk about ways to be kind to each other. Next ask children to share what they talked about and make a list of these ways to be kind on chart paper. Tell the children you will be noticing all the ways that they are kind to each other this week. Post the chart paper where it is easily seen and at the end of the day, describe the kind acts you saw that day. I do not recommend giving stickers or tangible items to children for being kind. We want to teach them that being kind is an expected way of behaving rather than something they get rewarded for.

Friendship Wishes

Gather the children together and have them turn and talk to their partner about what their friendship wishes are for the rest of the school year. Next have the children draw a picture or write about their wishes. See the worksheet below.

Super Friends Book

After you've discussed how to be kind, and talked about friendship wishes, ask the children what good friends do. Make a list. Using the worksheet below, have the children draw or write what they do to be a good friend. Put all the worksheets into a binder to create your class Super Friends Book.

Friendship Tree

Have the children trace their hands on green, yellow, red, or brown construction paper. Then have them cut it out (or you do it for them if they're too young). Next the children should write or dictate 3 or 4 things that good friends do. Make a bulletin board display in which you put the hands on a tree trunk to serve as leaves. Once a week, bring the children over to the bulletin board to read what they wrote on their hand.

March: Keeping My Body Still

Most young children and many older children have difficulty keeping their body still during lessons and throughout the day. The good news is that this skill can be taught. Over time, we can help children develop the muscle memory and self-awareness necessary to keep still. This is particularly important for helping children to focus and pay attention. As they are better able to control their body, they will be better able to control their attention and focus. Be sure, however, that your lessons are developmentally appropriate and you are not trying to keep children still for too long.

Freeze Games

An effective way to start body control is with old-fashioned freeze games. Put on music and stop the music randomly, having children freeze their body. You can also teach children to freeze at the sound of a chime and practice that throughout the day. Keep this fun and light hearted.

Stillness Time

Plan a time during the day when the whole class practices stillness time. I recommend starting this the first few times at the beginning of the day when children are not tired. Set a timer for 30 seconds and see if the children can last that long. Ask them to sit comfortably with their eyes closed. Some children will laugh and be silly at first because they are uncomfortable with the idea of stillness. Be serious yourself and remind the children that learning how to do this will help them be better students and learn more. Eventually, the children will take this more seriously. Stick with it long enough that children learn more self-control. Add another 30 seconds or minute to the amount of stillness time every few days until you are up to 5 minutes. Once the children can do this easily, use stillness time after lunch or recess or other times when children need to calm down.

Visual Support

Take a photo of each child when they are sitting quietly with their body in an appropriate position. Print out the photos and let the children glue them on index cards or tape them to their desks for reference.

Body Breaks

In order to keep our bodies still for longer periods of time, we all need to take short breaks. Think of these are "Body Breaks" like you might do "Brain Breaks." Teach the children how to take a short break. It might involve stretching their legs or arms for a moment, or getting a quick drink of water, or walking to the window and back.

Children who have a lot of difficulty staying still can keep a small timer at their desk. Set it for a minute or two and when it goes off, they can take a quick break (15 -30 seconds at most). Then they can set the timer again. Gradually increase the amount of time that they can work without a break. You can also give them 2 or 3 "Break Tickets" to use during the day that they can use to regulate the number of breaks they take.

Teaching How to Wait

We can teach children ways to make waiting easier. Model for the children ways to distract themselves - perhaps by counting, or singing to one's self, or looking around the room to find things that are interesting. Take opportunities throughout the day to remind children how to distract themselves. You can also teach them to say to themselves, "I can wait. I can wait. I can do it!" Some children may need extra help with this. During center time, you can work one-on-one with them, modeling again how to wait, and having them practice by pretending to be in different situations.

Social Skills Story for Children Who Struggle

One of the successful strategies to help children on the autism spectrum are individualized stories that help them learn skills. These stories can also be good for the whole class and especially for children with ADHD. Read the following story to the class and have them discuss it. Make a copy of the story for any of the children who might need extra support in keeping their body still. Read it to them one-on-one as needed and also let them take a copy home for their families to read to them. Leave a copy in your classroom library.

I Can Keep My Body Still

A Social Skills Story

Sometimes at school I have a hard time sitting still.

When I wiggle and get up and move around it's hard for me to pay attention.

When I move around I can't learn a lot and I bother the other children.

I can try hard to keep my body still.

I can look at the speaker.

I can squeeze my fidget ball.

I can take a deep breath.

If I really need a break, I can get a drink of water. Then I go back and sit down quickly and try again.

I learn a lot more when I keep my body still. I'm happy, the teacher is happy, and the other children are learning more, too!

THE END

April: Grit - How to Keep Going When Things Are Hard

Psychologists have found that the best predictor of success in challenging situations is something they call **GRIT**. This is the ability to keep going and not give up when things are difficult. Grit can be taught. The following activities will help start children on the path to persevere and succeed.

Teaching about Grit

Objective: Children will be able to describe the importance of working hard and not giving up.

Materials: A book about working hard such as *The Little Engine That Could*, *The Tortoise and the Hare*, *Heart of a Tiger* by Marsha Diane Arnold, or *A Boy Called Slow* by Joseph Bruchac.

Procedures:

1. Read *The Little Engine That Could* or a similar story about working hard. Discuss how the character eventually reached success. Emphasize the idea that working hard is more important than being smart. Bring up the idea that sometimes we want to give up and stop trying.

2. Have the children turn to their partner and discuss a time that they worked hard and didn't give up.

3. Let the children know that learning something new often requires hard work. It doesn't mean there's something wrong with them, but rather it's a normal part of learning. Make a chart with the children in which they come up with some of the negative thoughts they have and then come up with better things to say to themselves. See the example below, "What Can I Say to Myself?"

4. Have the children draw a picture of someone working hard, or have them write about a time they worked hard and didn't give up.

5. Hang up the "I Think I Can!" Poster and refer to it often this month. (See next page.)

What Can I Say to Myself?

This is too hard!	I can ask for help and I can work hard.
I'm too tired.	I can keep going for a little bit longer.
I can't do this.	I can figure out how to do this.
I'm not smart enough.	It's more important to work hard than be smart.
I make too many mistakes.	I can learn from my mistakes.
I'm bad at math.	I can get better at math if I work hard.
I'll never learn this!	I'll learn this if I keep working on it.

Self-Talk Cards

Sometimes the work gets hard, and children begin to get upset. Teach children ahead of time to use self-talk to calm down and keep going. Encourage children to control their emotional responses by having them repeat positive phrases to themselves. Create cards with phrases on them for reminders (See below). When children show signs of agitation, remind them to use self-talk and model for them.

I can do this.
I am calm.
I can keep going!
I can get better.
I am working hard.
I'll keep trying.

May: Self-Monitoring and Evaluation

Towards the end of the year, children can learn how to evaluate their own behavior. (This can also be done earlier in the year). Think of this as a gift that you will give to the teacher that the children have next year!

Objective: Children will be able to evaluate their own behavior.

Materials: Self-Monitoring Chart (see below)

Procedures:

1. Choose an activity that children are usually successful doing. Reading independently is a good choice. Explain that at the end of the activity the children will review how well they followed the appropriate behaviors and rate themselves. Show the children the self-evaluation form.

2. Conduct the activity and bring the children back to their desks, or give them clipboards with the chart on it.

3. The children should mark the appropriate rating for their behavior that day. Be sure they THEY rate themselves. Do not rate the children yourself. We are trying to teach self-evaluation.

Explain that they will continue to do this for the rest of the week. You can use this self-monitoring chart for any activity such as writing workshop, special classes outside the room, working together as a group, and so on.

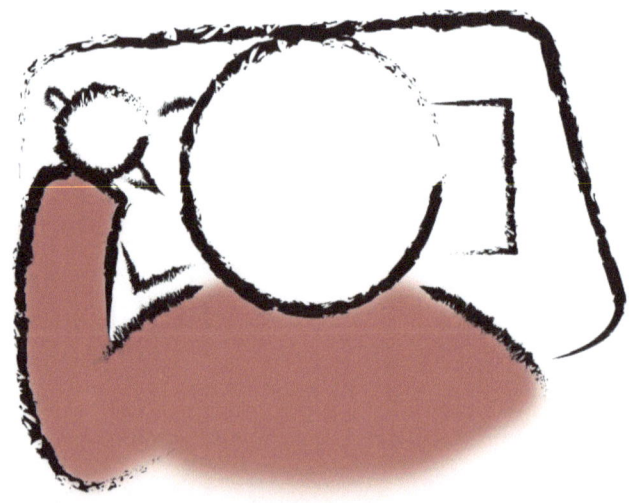

Self-Monitoring Chart

Behavior	Monday	Tuesday	Wednesday	Thursday	Friday
	☺ 😐 ☹	☺ 😐 ☹	☺ 😐 ☹	☺ 😐 ☹	☺ 😐 ☹
	☺ 😐 ☹	☺ 😐 ☹	☺ 😐 ☹	☺ 😐 ☹	☺ 😐 ☹
	☺ 😐 ☹	☺ 😐 ☹	☺ 😐 ☹	☺ 😐 ☹	☺ 😐 ☹
	☺ 😐 ☹	☺ 😐 ☹	☺ 😐 ☹	☺ 😐 ☹	☺ 😐 ☹

Classroom Management Master Calendar

Date	Procedures	Community-Building	School Success Skills
Sept, Week 1	• Quiet Signal • Arrival Procedures • Bathroom Routine • Lining Up • Walking in Hallway • Sitting at Group Time • Learner's Position • Dismissal Procedure • Putting Things Away in Desks • Getting a Drink • Fire Drills	All About Me Posters	Greetings and Manners
Sept, Week 2	• Voice Levels • Moving from Desks to Carpet • Moving from Carpet to Desks • Getting a Drink • Going to the Nurse • Sharpening Pencils • Classroom Jobs	Classmate BINGO	Saying Kind Words
Sept, Week 3	• Using Personal White Boards • Turn and Talk • Choral Response • Lock Down/Safety Drills • What to Do When You're Done Early	Focus Student of the Day	Calming Down
Sept, Week 4	• Reader's Workshop • Read to Self • Partner Reading • Listening Center • Writer's Workshop • Taking a Break • Math Centers	Classmate Survey: Getting to Know You	Tattling vs. Telling
October	• Learning Center Procedures • Done Early	• Classroom Spirit • Class T-Shirts • Name Games	Conflict Resolution

Month			
November	Review as needed	• Who Am I? • We Are Grateful Class Book • Comic Strip Fun	Staying Focused and Building Stamina
December	Review as needed	• What Do We Have in Common? • Secret Handshake • Holidays at Home	Sharing and Working Together
January	• Quiet Signal • Arrival Procedures • Bathroom Routine • Lining Up • Walking in Hallway • Sitting at Group Time • Learner's Position • Dismissal • Putting Things Away in Your Desk • Getting a Drink • Fire Drills	• Our Favorite Things • How Are We Doing? • Crazy Collaborative Creatures	Identifying, Labeling, and Expressing Feelings
February	Review as needed	• Puzzle Piece Valentine's Game • Musical Hoola Hoops • Back-to-Back Drawing	Being a Good Friend
March	Review as needed	• Reader's Theater • Inside/Outside Circles • We're All Superheroes	Keeping My Body Still
April	Review as needed	• Partner Obstacle Course • Pat on the Back • The Wave	Grit: How to Keep Going When Things Are Hard
May	Review as needed	• What's the Difference? • How Does Your Garden Grow? • Parachute Games	Self-Monitoring and Evaluation
June	Review as needed	• End-of-Year Class Book • End-of-Year Award Ceremony • End-of-Year Read-Alouds	

Part 4:

Techniques for Engaging Learners

Engaging Learners

The easiest way to make sure that children behave is to fully engage them during lessons. There are two strategies to do this:

1. Lesson format: Work with small groups or one-on-one
2. Lesson strategies: Use engagement strategies during whole group activities

The rest of this section will provide techniques for both of these strategies so you can get your children to focus, pay attention, and behave well during your lessons.

Lesson Format

Whole group lessons are not as effective as small group or individual lesson because the children are all at slightly different learning levels (or vastly different learning levels). Behavior problems arise when children are not challenged by the lesson or when the lesson is over their heads. The solution? Turn your whole group lessons into small group or individual lessons. Here's how:

Using Learning Centers, Stations, or Groups

1. **Mini-Lessons: 7-10 minutes.** Cut down your whole group lesson into a 7-10 minute mini-lesson by presenting only the instructional part of the lesson. This should focus on one skill or concept. Children cannot easily process more information than this, so we waste a lot of time in longer lessons.
2. **Guided Practice: 15-20 minutes.** Have the children work in ability groups on guided practice with the skill or concept you taught. Different groups can be working at different levels or on different needed skills. You can work with one group to provide extra support while the other groups work independently. Work with a different group each rotation.
3. **Repeat.** This cycle of mini lesson and guided practice can be repeated for longer blocks of time.

The trick to using learning centers or stations effectively is to think through the procedures and teach each one carefully. Be sure you've taught most of your basic procedures (such as quiet signal, transitions, etc.) beofre starting learning centers. See STEP 1 for more information on learning center procedures and planning. The next few pages have some forms to help you think through the procedures for your learning centers.

Planning Learning Centers

Free Choice Centers

The children are allowed to choose any center, although there may be limits on how many students can be in each center. The children can also choose when they switch to another activity.

Teacher Planned Centers

Children are assigned to a group and then the group is assigned to a specific center. After a set period of time, usually 15-20 minutes, the children move to the next center. One of the centers is usually a small group activity with the teacher.

Mixed Choice Centers

Children are given a choice of what center to start at (again, with limits on the number of children at certain centers); however, there are certain centers that must be done each day, or certain center activities they must complete by the end of the week.

What are good center activities?

Any learning activity that children can do independently (that is, without your help) will work as a center activity. This could be a mandatory worksheet, although hands-on activities are more engaging and more effective for learning. Check your curriculum guides and look at the guided practice or independent practice activities. You can have children do these at centers instead. The benefit is that children can spend as much or little time as they need and can then work on something else. They can also collaborate, if you want them to.

Examples of learning center activities:
- Read to yourself/Read with a partner
- Writing activities with prompts or templates
- Math games with or without partners
- Computer or tablet activities
- Commercial learning games (such as Lakeshore)
- Games or activities on the interactive white board (SmartBoard)
- Simple science experiments
- Social studies readings & responses, such as Time for Kids, or Newsela

Center Time Planning Sheet

Type of Centers: ___ Free Choice   ___ Teacher Planned   ___ Mixed Choice

List of Centers Available:

1. _____
2. _____
3. _____
4. _____
5. _____
6. _____

Center Assignments (for Teacher Planned Centers)

Learning Center Activity Plan

Name of Center:

Objectives:

Level of difficulty: ☐ Beginner ☐ Intermediate ☐ Advanced

Materials needed:

Procedures:

Assessment:

Center Time Procedures Planning Sheet

➢ How long will each center rotation be?

➢ What do children do if they need help?

➢ Where do children record their work or hand it in?

➢ What do children do if they finish early?

➢ How will children move to the next center?

Making Seatwork Successful

Careful planning of seatwork can help you avoid behavior problems and children being off-task. See the strategies below and the signs on the next few pages.

Give Clear Directions

Be sure you are giving the directions clearly and simply. Don't overwhelm children with too many things to remember. Provide visual prompts or examples as much as possible. Use Turn and Talk to have children review the directions before dismissing the children to work independently.

Seating

Some children are too easily distracted to be able to focus with other children next to them. Try to provide seating away from others at a table at the back of the room, or allow children to move their desks apart during seatwork. Do not penalize children by moving their desk away from others; this should be presented as a helpful strategy rather than a punishment. They can move desks together for group work later. You can also provide cardboard study carrols to provide privacy.

Asking for Help

You should be using seatwork time to confer individually with children or work with small groups. Therefore, you need to teach children not to interrupt you during this time. Create a set of procedures to ensure this goes smoothly. You can use a STOP sign to remind children not to bother you. Teaching children to "Ask 3 Before Me" will help them be independent without you. You can also designate one of your weekly jobs to a few students who help others during work times. "Ask Me" badges or necklaces will show who they can consult. Some teachers also designate children to help with technology problems. See the signs and badges below.

Plan for Children Who Finish Early

Children often demonstrate inappropriate behavior when they don't have anything to do. Plan simple activities that children can do when they finish their work. Create task cards, put ideas on a bulletin board, keep bins of materials ready, or give each child a folder of activities to keep in their desk. See the labels below to use on a bulletin board to remind children of their choices.

- Read a book
- Write a story
- Do a puzzle
- Complete a math worksheet
- Play a math game
- Write in your journal
- Work on your writing piece
- Help a friend
- Work on the computer
- Clean out your desk

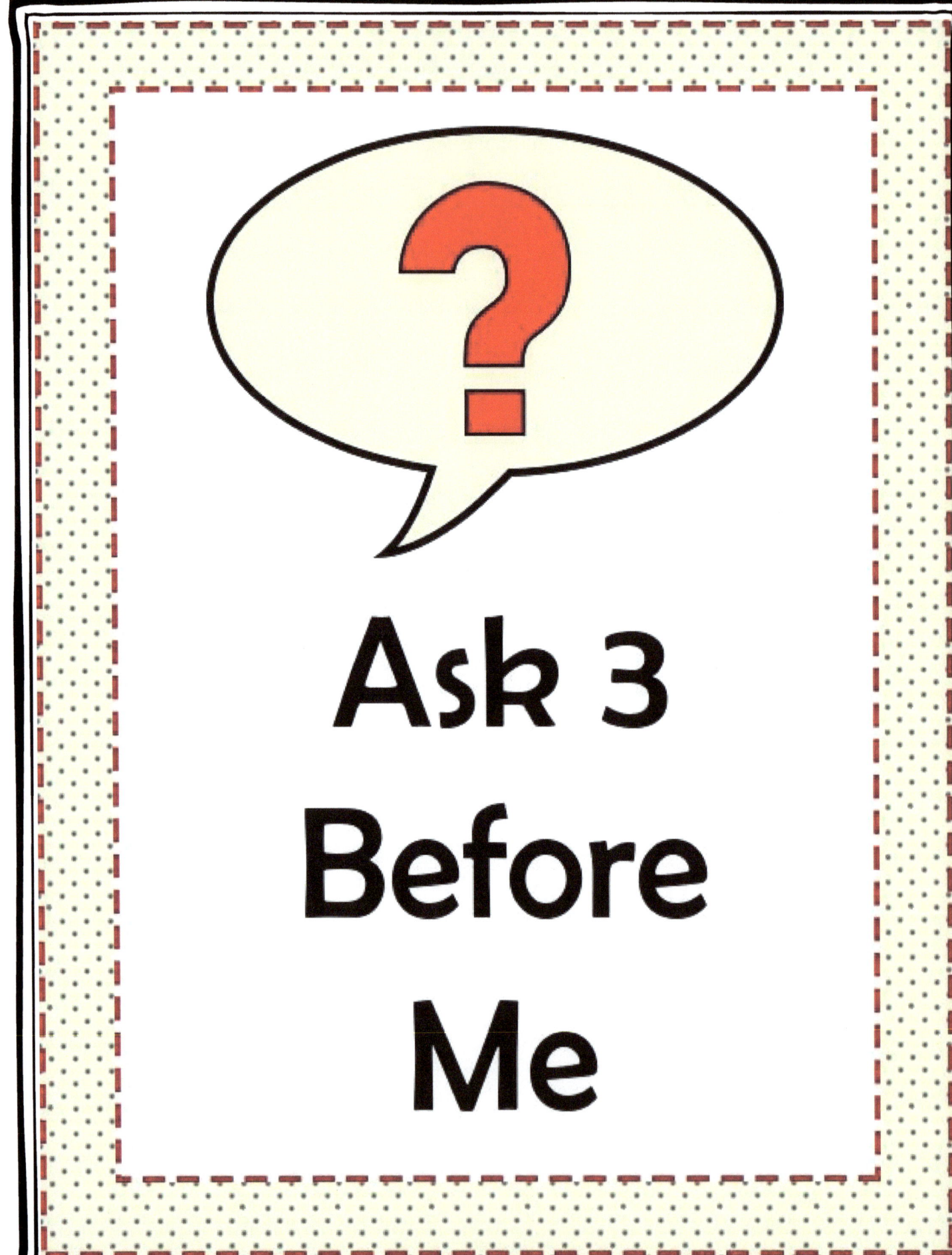

Do Not Disturb

Teacher Working

Helper Badges/Necklaces

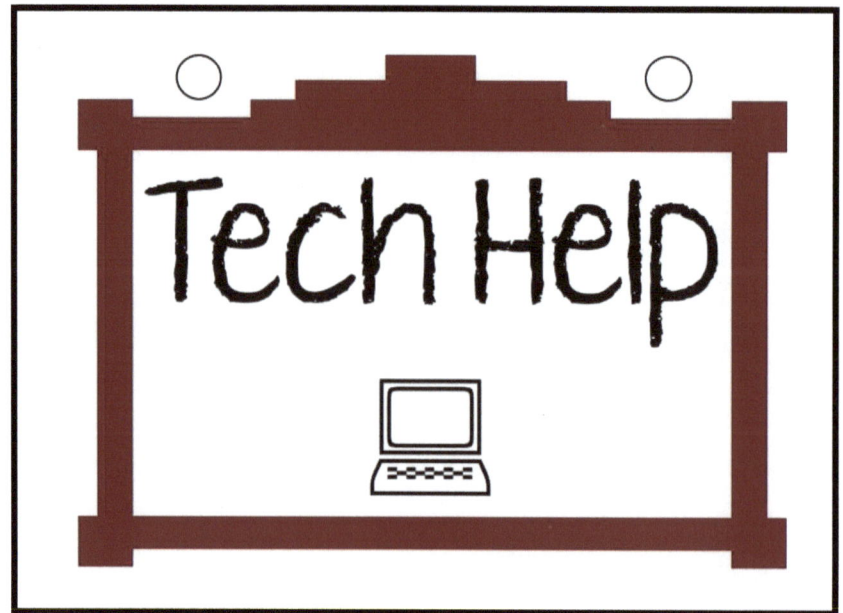

"I'm Done!" Bulletin Board Labels

Read A Book

Write A Story

Do A Puzzle

Complete A Math Worksheet

Play A Math Game

- Write In Your Journal
- Work On Your Writing Piece
- Help A Friend
- Work On The Computer
- Clean Out Your Desk

Alternatives to Hand-Raising

Asking children to answer questions by raising their hands is a very ineffective way of engaging learners. Many young children do not have the self-control to learn this routine, and the children who don't get to answer don't learn much. Children learn by answering, talking, writing, doing. Instead of hand-raising, try the following techniques instead. Be sure to teach the procedures for each one carefully before trying them out!

Turn and Talk

After the question is asked, pairs of children turn to each other. One listens while the other answers. This way half of the class is engaged in talking, and it is easier for children to pay attention to the speaker in a paired situation. Be sure that children know ahead of time who their partner is and have them practice how to pair up. This should move quickly, so keep the pace brisk. This works well for reading lessons when you want children to think and share their ideas.

Choral responses

To increase student engagement and reinforce simple concepts, allow the children to respond all together. This works best for questions with one answer, and as a quick review of previously covered material. You can cue children to respond with a hand signal.

Cold call

Keep a list of children's names or put their names on cards, or sticks, and randomly pick children's names to answer. This helps to improve the pace of the lesson, and keeps children engaged and ready to answer since they don't know when they will be called on. It also ensures that all children get a chance to participate and a few children are not dominating the discussions. Keep it positive. This should not be humiliating or embarrassing. Make sure that the children are able to be successful with the content you are reviewing.

Individual whiteboards

Each child has a whiteboard and marker and they write down their answer to the question. Children hold up their boards so the teacher can judge how well the they are understanding the concepts. This works especially well for math problems.

Post the following sign in your group meeting area to remind you to try these different techniques, especially when you see the children are starting to lose focus.

Alternatives to Hand Raising

Turn and Talk

Choral Responses

Cold Calling

Individual White Boards

Turn and Talk

Use these visual cues to help children learn the procedures for Turn and Talk. Hold up the Turn and Talk sign to cue them to begin. For practice, you can copy enough TALK and LISTEN cards for all the children. One child holds the listen card, the other holds the talk card. After practicing, the children switch cards.

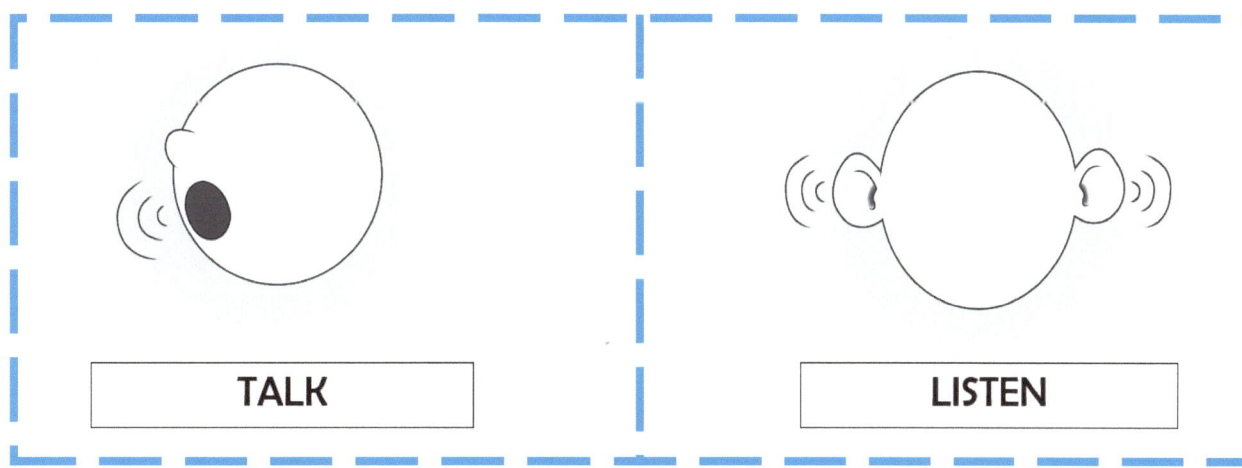

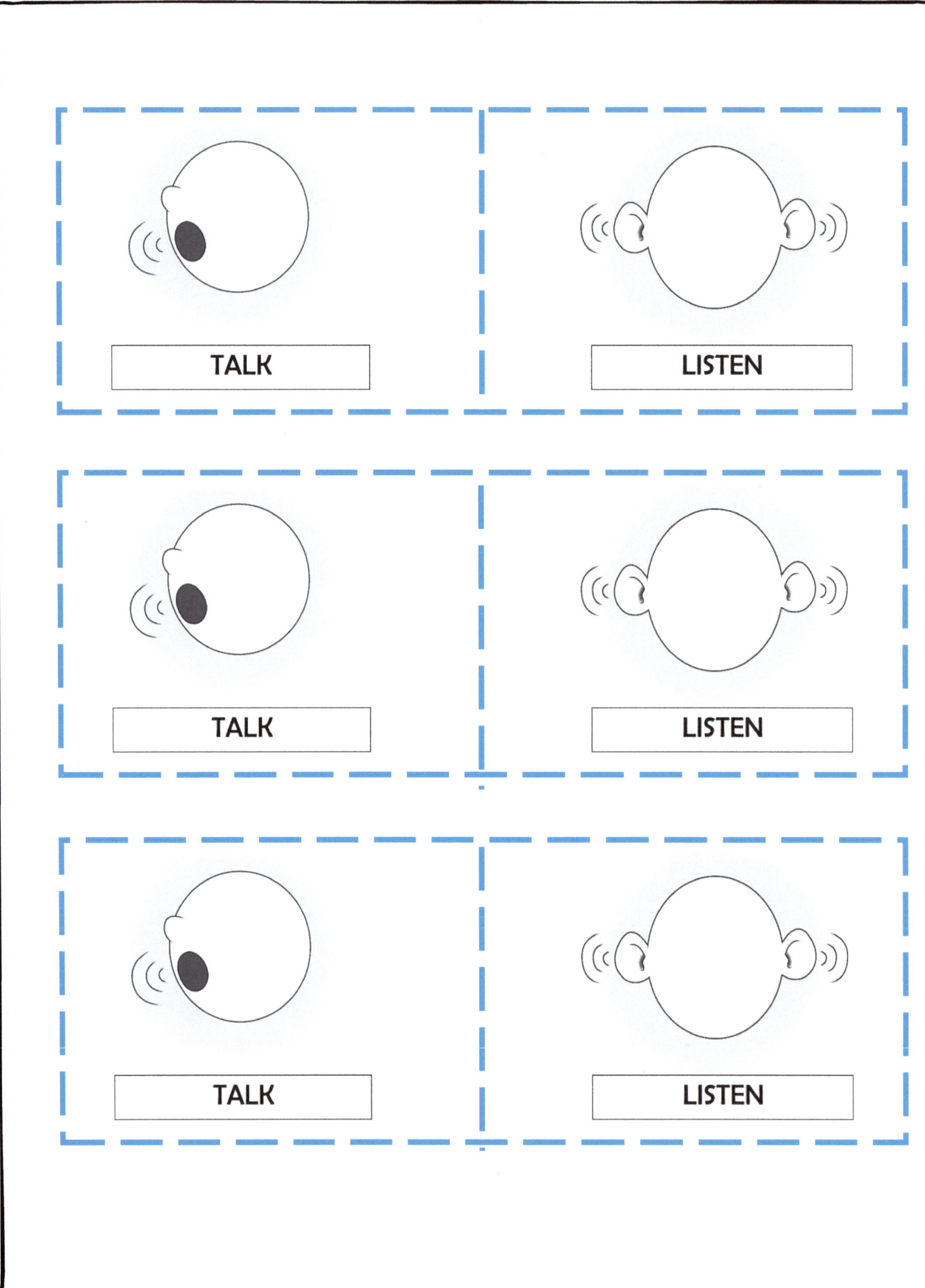

Cold Calling Name Cards

Choral Response Cards

Think

Respond

Asking Engaging Questions

Use the following cards to help you develop effective questions. Write them out ahead of time and put them on index cards or post-it notes so you have them ready.

Remembering

- What is….?
- Who…?
- Can you describe…?
- What happened…?
- What do you remember about…?
- What is the answer to…?
- How many…..were there?
- Where did the story take place?
- What happened next?

Understanding

- Can you put this in your own words?
- What is the main idea?
- Why….?
- Can you summarize this?
- Turn to a partner and explain…
- What are you confused about?
- What questions do you have?
- Why did you choose that answer?

Applying

- Have you ever felt like this character?
- What would you do in this situation?
- When else can we use this strategy?
- Can you apply this method to a different question?
- How would you use…?
- What questions would you ask…?
- Has this ever happened to you?
- Try using your partner's ideas. Do they work?

Analyzing (Breaking Apart)

- How does this compare to…?
- What part do you like best?
- How is this story the same as (or different than) …?
- What are the most important ideas in this text?
- Why did the author choose these words?
- How is this version of the story similar to….?
- Which of these events could have really happened?
- How did you figure that out?

Creating (Synthesizing)

- Can you create a new ending for the story?
- How else could you solve this?
- What dialogue would your character say?
- What happens next in your story?
- How else can you use this?
- What else could this character do?
- Can you draw a picture of what happened?
- How can you test this?

Evaluating (Critiquing)

- How well did you do this?
- Which book did you like better? Why?
- Which strategy worked better? Why?
- What changes would you recommend?
- Was that a good idea?
- Did he/she make a good decision?
- What would make this better?
- Would you recommend this text? Why?

Being Prepared

Children often misbehave because the teacher is not ready for the activity. Children left sitting on the rug, or waiting at desks or tables will find something to do that you might not like, and then you have to work harder to get their attention back. Adapt the following form to help you plan your day so that you have no wait time for the children.

Daily To Do List

Tasks Before Children Arrive:

Morning Materials Needed:

Tasks During Prep Time:

Afternoon Materials Needed:

Part 5: Strategies for Guiding Behavior

Guiding Children's Behavior

Instead of punishment or "discipline," think about guiding children's behavior by teaching them better choices. Simply put, punishment is not effective for changing behavior in the long run, and it can lead to humiliation and emotional pain.

Behavior can be understood as a form of communication. Instead of jumping to the conclusion that the child is wrong, it is helpful first to look at the social, physical, academic and emotional environment in the classroom. Have the children been sitting too long? Is the space too crowded? Are the activities too challenging? Not challenging enough? Is the child hungry, tired, or not feeling well? A great deal of inappropriate behavior occurs because of the classroom context, not because there is  something deficient in the child. Sometimes our efforts as teachers cause inappropriate behavior from children. That's why it's so important to teach procedures, build community and teach school success skills first. Don't jump into trying to correct student behavior without a thorough review of your own classroom practices.

What about the parents?

Don't children misbehave because they haven't been disciplined or taught how to behave at home? That's probably true, but the parents are also probably not able to help you. You absolutely can teach a child to behave properly in school, even if they go home to an environment that is not supportive. Children learn at a very early age that they need to behave differently at grandma's house, for example, than at home. They can also learn to behave appropriately at school. In fact, parents can only help so much, because the problem behavior is happening at school. Just like you can't easily teach children to clean up their room, or be polite at the dinner table because you are not there, parents can't easily help their children learn school behaviors. Instead, create a plan of what behaviors a child needs help with and let parents know what you are doing in school to help. You can suggest some behaviors the children can practice at home (such as calming down, or using words instead of hitting), but remember that you are the trained professional, and parents often don't have the skills you'd expect. Teach them and offer help, without assigning blame or demanding they "fix" their child's problems. For more help with serious behavior problems, consult *The Positive Classroom* by Muriel Rand or look into other resources focused on Positive Behavior Support.

In this section of the Field Guide are classroom strategies to help you deal with typical misbehaviors that arise as children test their limits and begin to develop self-regulation.

Responding to Student Behavior

What do you do when children misbehave? How do you respond when children test you or make inappropriate choices of behavior? This section of the Field Guide will offer a variety of strategies to help you set boundaries, keep a positive climate, and respond to misbehavior in positive ways that teach children how to behave better.

Pick Your Battles

You don't have to respond to every misbehavior in your classroom. Often children will self-correct or peers will help to correct children. Think about these possible responses:

Looking On
Observe children to see if they can fix the problem themselves. They may regain focus, solve conflicts, or redirect themselves on their own.

Proximity
Move closer to the child while still teaching. No talking is necessary. Your presence acts as a reminder of the behavior that is expected.

Reminders
Give short reminders (all eyes should be on me) or use visuals to cue children. Don't focus on the negative; just remind children of what they should be doing.

Redirecting
Ask the child to go to the Quiet Corner or get a drink. Redirect them to another task, or ask them to help you. Focus on getting them to do a positive task rather than discussing the negative.

Stopping
Maintain safety as needed. Calmly remove a child from the situation. DO NOT raise your voice or show anger. The calmer you are, the more effective your response will be.

Least Intervention ↑↓ Most Intervention

Positive Teacher Language: Your Secret Weapon!

The best way to get children to behave properly is by giving them positive feedback and praise. This is the most powerful tool in your toolbox and it's almost impossible to use it too much. In the best-run classrooms, teachers are continually narrating the positive.

Positive Feedback

"I see three children have their books out and open." "Marcia and Judy, you shared your materials well today." This is encouraging talk that describes the positive things your children are doing. It shows that you are interested in their work and efforts and it provides clear feedback to the children about what they are doing right. It helps children to behave!!

Empty Praise

Short comments like, "good job" and "nice work" feel good and create a positive environment, and are fine once in a while. However, children don't learn much from them about why they did a good job, or what aspect of their work is good. They are like junk food – they taste good, but are not very nutritious. Use them sparingly for quick feedback.

Manipulative Praise

"I like the way David is sitting." Children quickly learn that these statements are coercive and are not sincere. They pit one child against the others and can lead to resentment. Instead, try describing what children are doing that is appropriate in an anonymous way: "Some children are ready, sitting quietly on the rug with legs crossed."

Negative Nagging

"Jared, stop that." "No calling out." "You were all very noisy in the hall." "Shhh!" These statements give children attention for the wrong behaviors. Even worse, they don't let the children know what they *should* be doing. Instead, use positive feedback to focus on what your expectations are. If a child needs correction, do it privately.

Humiliation

"You'll never make to 3rd grade if you keep that up." "Who do you think you are?" "What's wrong with you?" These statements are never appropriate and come from extreme frustration – a sign that a teacher needs plenty of work on her own emotional regulation. These comments encourage children to become defensive and act out, or be humiliated and shut down. They create a poor learning environment.

Post the following chart on your wall to help you remember to use positive feedback. Try practicing using more positive language throughout the day – and especially when things get chaotic.

Teacher Language Scale

Positive Feedback
"I see three children have their books out and open."
"You shared your materials well today."
"You were very helpful to your friends at this table"

Empty Praise
"Nice work, Marcia."
"Good job."
"Your painting is beautiful."

Manipulative Praise
"I like the way David is sitting."
"Thank you, Keisha, for paying attention."

Nagging
"Jared, stop doing that."
"Stop calling out."
"Shhhh!"

Humiliation
"You'll never make it to 3rd grade if you keep that up."
"Who do you think you are?"
"What's wrong with you?"

The Positive Classroom   ©thepositiveclassroom.org

Intervening in the Acting Out Cycle

In order to understand children's challenging behaviors, it's helpful to take a closer look at what is going on when children act out with behaviors such as screaming, throwing things, fighting, or tantrums. It may seem like this behavior comes out of nowhere, but we can identify phases in this acting out cycle that are predictable (The IRIS Center: http://iris.peabody.vanderbilt.edu/module/bi1/). When you learn to identify the phases in this cycle, you can intervene earlier and prevent the child from losing control.

The figure below shows the seven steps of the acting out cycle, demonstrating how the intensity builds and accelerates into a peak, and then subsides. Your goal is to help the child in the early stages of the cycle, preventing the peak from occuring. Your response to the child's acting out cycle will completely depend on what point in the cycle you are intervening.

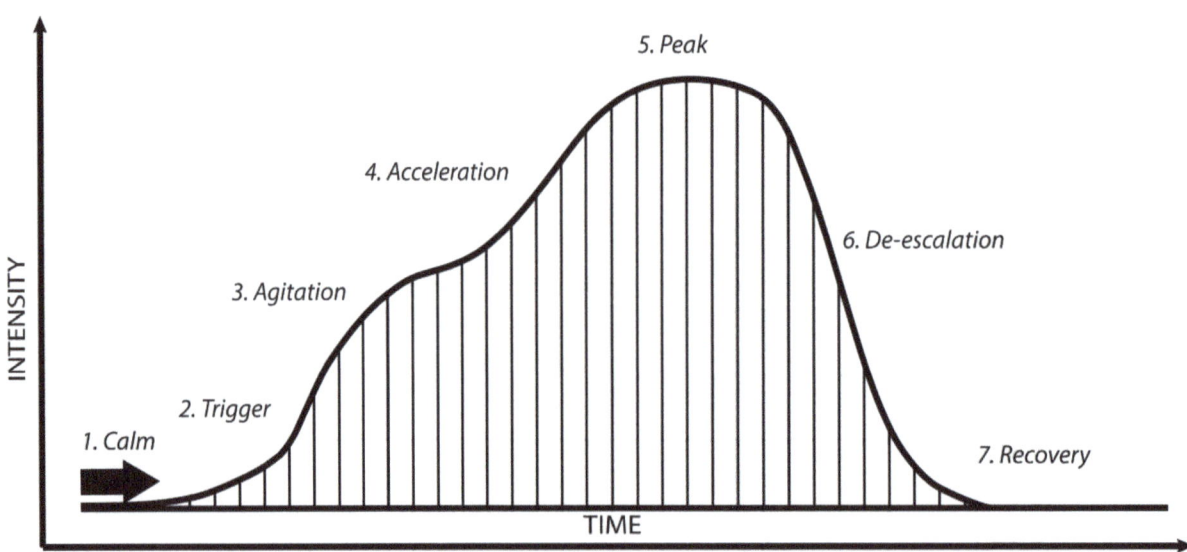

The Acting Out Cycle

Phase	Student Behavior	Teacher Response
1. Calm	Children are engaged fully in learning activity; emotional stability and full cognitive focus.	Provide positive attention, work on developing relationships with children, provide safe, calm environment.
2. Trigger	Environmental stressors such as change in schedule, boredom, confusion, over-stimulation, negative social interactions; internal stressors such as hunger, lack of sleep, illness, medication, stress at home.	Begin to recognize what triggers are and help to prevent them, change the setting or social interactions, offer positive attention.
3. Agitation Phase	Disengages from activity or lesson; shows body movements of agitation—tapping, rocking, running around—or stares into space, walks around unengaged, stops participating.	Redirect child, change the way the child is working on the activity—offer choices; provide assistance, offer calming techniques.
4. Acceleration Phase	Attempts to gain teacher attention in negative ways: argues, is non-compliant, tests limits, tries to provoke the teacher and/or other children.	Redirect child to appropriate behavior calmly, acknowledge feelings, make high-probability requests; give positive attention. Do not engage in argument, use sarcasm, or offer negative remarks.
5. Peak Phase	Child is out of control; verbal and physical aggression toward teacher and other children; crying, damaging materials.	Maintain safety, stay calm yourself, help child to regain control in a respectful, caring way.
6. De-escalation Phase	Child is disoriented, confused, tired, and often withdrawn; typically receptive to teacher requests; may blame others and try to reconcile.	Move child to Quiet Corner, provide calm independent activity; check on the rest of class to restore order.
7. Recovery Phase	Child is subdued and has calmed down. May avoid talking about the incident.	Debriefing of incident is critical. Discuss what triggered incident and make plan for prevention in future.

From The IRIS Center for Training Enhancements: http://iris.peabody.vanderbilt.edu/module/bi1/

Using a Quiet Corner

Children need a positive place to calm down and gain self-control. Create a warm, comforting space in your classroom and give it a name such as, "Quiet Corner." Choose a place in the room such as a comfortable chair, carpet square, pillows, or other spot that is removed from the action, but not really isolated.

Help the children understand the purpose of this place. Explain that we all need help from time to time in learning how to make good choices. We have strong impulses that make us choose what we want to do instead of what we have to do. Going to the Quiet Corner is for a short period to calm down and think about a better choice.

Model for the children how the Quiet Corner will work. You might want to give a child a brief reminder of appropriate behavior before sending a child to the Quiet Corner and then if the behavior reoccurs, a Quiet Corner signal should be used. Children can also choose to use the Quiet Corner when they need to calm themselves down, or to get away for a minute or two. Obviously, you should not let children "escape" in the Quiet Corner and avoid academic activities, but it can be very helpful in getting a child to relax and get back to work. Also teach the class how to help someone who is taking a break by leaving him alone and continuing one's work.

Once you've modeled this process, have the children practice it. You can go to the Quiet Corner as well, to get across the idea that we all need support at times. Model what a child should be doing when taking a break. Teach children how to take deep breaths to calm their bodies and minds. Pretend to be in the Quiet Corner and model your thinking out loud, especially calming down, gaining control, and making a good choice.

The most critical aspect of using the Quiet Corner as a positive process is your attitude and tone of voice. Children can tell when you are annoyed and frustrated and then this will turn into an ineffective punishment. You don't want this to be Time-Out.

Be sure to welcome the child back to the class activities in a positive way. Show the child that he is cared for and an important part of the group and get the child involved in work right away. Some children might need a discussion with you later about why they needed a break and how they might behave more appropriately in the future. The focus should always be on what better choice the child can make. Instead of "think about what you did" the child should be encouraged to "calm down and think about what you need to do now."

Calm-Down Kit

Gather some of the following materials together and put them in a plastic box or basket. Keep the Calm-Down Kit in your Quiet Corner and teach the children how to use the items. When a children are upset, direct them to choose an activity from the Calm-Down Kit to relax and recover their self-control.

Materials:

- Anger Choice Board (See below)
- Squeeze ball
- Plastic Snow-Globe (Child shakes it and watches the glitter settle)
- Playdough
- Photo cards of beautiful places
- Flower and Candle Breathing Card (See Part 3)
- 5 Breaths Card (See Part 3)
- Crayons and pad of drawing paper
- Self-Talk Cards on a binder ring
- Small stuffed animals
- Pinwheel

Anger Choice Board

Place a copy of the Anger Choice Board in your Quiet Corner or Calm-Down Kit. You can also cut out each square and put them on a binder ring for a child to keep at his/her desk.

Anger Choice Board

Breathe Deeply	Get a Drink	Draw a Picture

Count to 10	Think About a Happy Place	Listen to Music

Hug a Stuffed Animal	Read a Book	Use a Squeeze Ball
		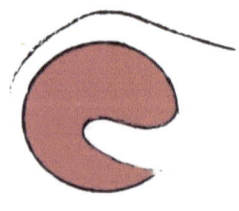
Look Out the Window	Use the Glitter Bottle	Ask for a Hug
	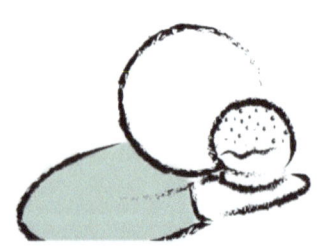	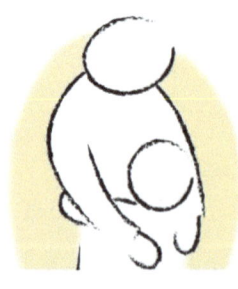

Setting and Enforcing Limits

It is your job as a teacher to let children know when their behavior is not appropriate. This is sometimes difficult for new teachers because they are afraid of "being mean" to the children and not being liked. Rest assured, though, that you do not need to scream, punish or be mean in order to set limits. In fact, children will appreciate knowing that someone will help them learn control because it is a frightening world when any behavior is allowed. Limits on behavior help children develop a personal understanding of what is right and wrong. Always be careful that children are not humiliated. The focus should be on what the child can learn, rather than punishment.

Exclusion (Can't Participate)

When children are not able to adhere to the behaviors needed to participate in social activities, you can exclude them as a way of teaching them the boundaries for the behavior. Here are some examples:

Leave the sandbox: Keyana is sitting in the sandbox and she excitedly throws the sand up in the air over and over again. You rush over. "Keyana, you must stop throwing the sand in the air, it can hurt children's eyes. We don't hurt others." A few minutes later you see Keyana return to her previous actions, throwing the sand higher. You say to her in a calm tone, "Keyana, I see you are having a hard time playing safely with the sand. You will need to leave the sandbox so our friends are all safe. Tomorrow you can try again to see if you can play safely." You help Keyana choose a different activity, gently guiding her out of the sandbox.

Go to the Quiet Corner. Brian came back after lunch very irritable and had been arguing with his classmates during center time. His teacher reminded him twice about working cooperatively and modeled positive things to say. A few minutes later, Brian pushed Michael and knocked off some of the materials on the table. The teacher calmly approached and said, "Brian, it looks like you are frustrated and angry (acknowledging feelings). I can't let you disturb the other children who are working or damage our materials. Please go to the Quiet Corner until you feel ready to join the group again." Notice that his teacher did not impose a time limit on how long he needed to stay there. This was a powerful way of giving control back to Brian and allowing him to practice self-regulating.

Deprivation (Can't Use Materials)

An effective way to teach children how to treat materials is to take away the opportunity to use them for a short while. First, make sure that children know what behaviors are expected. Next, they need to know that you are serious about the expectations and that you will enforce them. As always, this needs to be done without any anger or frustration in your voice. Think of this as teaching the limits of behavior rather than punishment. Here are some examples:

Using markers correctly. A first-grade teacher was having a difficult time getting Hannah to remember to put the covers on the markers. After repeated attempts to show her how to make sure the caps are on and clicked shut, Hannah was still tossing the markers into the bin on her table without the covers on. Her teacher approached her and said in a calm voice, "Hannah, I see you are having trouble using the markers properly. I can't let them be ruined since everyone enjoys them. Today you will need to use your pencil or crayons instead. We'll try the markers again this afternoon to see if you are able to take care of them." The teacher moved the markers away, and put down a pack of crayons next to her.

Flying rubber-bands. Jake was enthusiastic about using the geoboards to make patterns during math. Even when shown the proper way to use the rubber bands, he continued to shoot them around the room. His teacher, Ms. Winston, gently took away the board and rubber bands. "Jake, you haven't yet learned how to use the geoboards properly so today you can use paper and pencil to make your patterns. Tomorrow we will try again to see if you can use the rubber bands safely so that no-one gets hurt."

Restitution (Fix What You Did Wrong)

Teach children how to make amends when they have made the wrong choices in their behaviors. Rather than punishing a child for an action, it's a better learning experience for them to see that they have caused a problem and should then fix it. This strategy can be applied to a wide variety of situations, such as when one child hurts another child. Restitution can also be used in conjunction with the other strategies described above. Here are some examples:

Make someone feel better. Annie has just knocked over Frankie's block structure as she dashed through the block area in her preschool. Her teacher gently stops her and points out that she has damaged Frankie's work. "See, Frankie is very sad that all his work has been knocked down because you rushed through this area. What can you do to make Frankie feel better?" Perhaps Annie will offer to help Frankie rebuild the structure, or give him a hug. The teacher asked Frankie what would work best for him and then guided Annie in following up on her restitution.

Fix what is broken. After Asad ripped one of the classroom books in anger, the teacher calmly dealt with his behavior (by teaching breathing strategies for him to calm down before he gets so angry) and had Asad tape the pages of the book to fix them.

When you use any kind of consequences, be sure you use a calm, matter-of-fact voice and be sure that the child understands the cause and effect relationship. **Never use sarcasm, humiliation, or harm.** Your message must be that the behavior is unacceptable, but the child is cared about. Continue to work on building and maintaining a strong relationship with the child, even when using consequences. If you find that you have strong emotions building up, use a calming technique for yourself before intervening.

Reducing Attention-Seeking Behavior

"Ignore him—he just wants attention!" Attention seeking behavior has a bad reputation in our schools, and it can often lead to difficult classroom management challenges. Seeking attention is a way of getting our love and belongingness needs met. The need for human interaction and affection is so strong that it is a kind of hunger—the more a child lacks these interactions, the harder he will try to get them. Any interactions, even negative ones, are better than none.

Many children act out in order to get the social interaction with the teacher that they need. Often a child with frequent misbehavior is sent to a vice principal, center director, or other disciplinarian, where he gets additional one-on-one attention. In any case, the typical result of attention-seeking behavior is, not surprisingly, lots of attention!

So wouldn't it make sense to ignore these behaviors to stop reinforcing them? Yes, but only if you *increase* the amount of positive attention the child gets at other times. The child is hungry for a relationship with you and it can be difficult to develop this if you are angry and frustrated with the child. What to do instead?

Here's the 4-step plan:

1. Plan for One-on-One Attention
2. Use Buddy Activities
3. Send Positive Notes Home
4. Enlist Other Adults for Attention

Use the worksheet on the next page to make a plan for the children in your classroom who need help with attention-seeking behavior.

Worksheet for Helping Attention-Seeking Children

1. Schedule time

Plan when you will be able to spend time with the child. Sit next to him at snack or invite him to read to you one-on-one. Greet him warmly when he arrives and spend an extra minute talking with him at the end of the day. Have honest, authentic interactions. Find out more about his likes, habits, fears, and hopes. Think about connecting.

Interactions planned:
_____
_____

Time of interactions: _____

2. Plan social interactions

Plan ways he can interact with other children in a successful way. Pair him up with a child who has excellent social skills for buddy activities.

Possible Buddies:
_____
_____

Buddy Activities:
_____
_____
_____

3. Send home positive notes

Once a week, send a note that describes a couple of positive things that the child did that week. Do not share the minor negative issues.

Day to send note home weekly: _____

4. Help connect child to other adults

Ask the child to bring a note to the office, help the teacher assistant set up lunch, or spend time with the social worker, security guard, or the librarian.

Plan for Connecting to Other Adults:
_____
_____

Summary

The Positive Classroom Field Guide will help you create a joyful, smooth-running classroom where the children are on task and learning. If you are a new teacher, following these steps can help you learn the basics of classroom management easily. If you an experienced teacher with a difficult class, these activities can help you create a positive learning environment.

If you'd like to print out this guide please request a FREE electronic copy by forwarding a copy of your receipt to info@thepositiveclassroom.org.

Best wishes for a successful school year that is filled with the deep satisfaction of helping children grow and learn!

For more teaching ideas and the Positive Classroom Method Online Training Course, visit thepositiveclassroom.org

www.ingramcontent.com/pod-product-compliance
Lightning Source LLC
Chambersburg PA
CBHW040907020526
44114CB00038B/80